DUNSTABLE IN 50 BUILDINGS

PAUL RABBITTS

AMBERLEY

To Marie, who has never been to Dunstable, and is unlikely to ever do so, but to whom I will always be grateful for her generosity, kindness and compassion.

First published 2024

Amberley Publishing, The Hill, Stroud
Gloucestershire GL5 4EP

www.amberley-books.com

British Library Cataloguing in Publication Data.
A catalogue record for this book is available from the British Library.

ISBN 978 1 3981 0404 4 (print)
ISBN 978 1 3981 0405 1 (ebook)

Typesetting by SJmagic DESIGN SERVICES, India.
Printed in Great Britain.

Contents

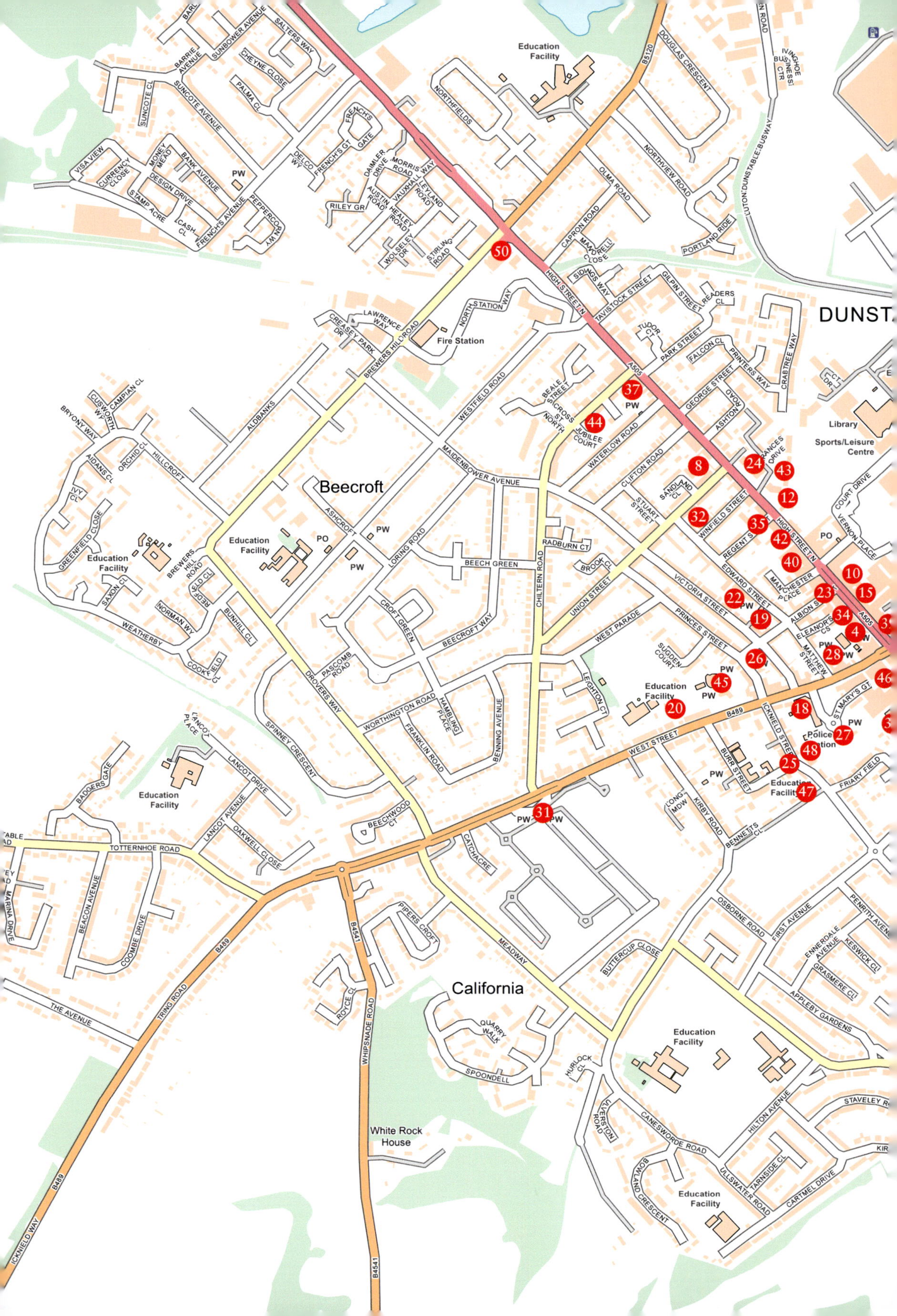

DUNST
Beecroft
California
Education Facility
Fire Station
Library
Sports/Leisure Centre
Police Station
White Rock House
PW
PO
HIGH STREET N
A505
B5120
B489
B4541
WEST STREET
TRING ROAD
ICKNIELD WAY
WHIPSNADE ROAD
MEADWAY
DROVERS WAY
BREWERS HILL ROAD
CHILTERN ROAD
WESTFIELD ROAD
MAIDENBOWER AVENUE
UNION STREET
VICTORIA STREET
PRINCES STREET
EDWARD STREET
WINFIELD STREET
CLIFTON ROAD
WATERLOW ROAD
GEORGE STREET
ASHTON ROAD
PARK STREET
TAVISTOCK STREET
GILPIN STREET
NORTHVIEW ROAD
DOUGLAS CRESCENT
OLMA ROAD
CAPRON ROAD
NORTHFIELDS
TOTTERNHOE ROAD
LANCOT DRIVE
LANCOT AVENUE
OAKWELL CLOSE
BEACON AVENUE
COOMBE DRIVE
MARINA DRIVE
THE AVENUE
SPINNEY CRESCENT
WORTHINGTON ROAD
FRANKLIN ROAD
BENNING AVENUE
BEECROFT WAY
CROFT GREEN
LORING ROAD
BEECH GREEN
ASHCROFT
ALDBANKS
HILLCROFT
WEATHERBY
GREENFIELD CLOSE
CANESWORDE ROAD
ULLSWATER ROAD
HILTON AVENUE
OSBORNE ROAD
FIRST AVENUE
APPLEBY GARDENS
BOWLAND CRESCENT
KIRBY ROAD
BURR STREET
ICKNIELD STREET
CATCHACRE
PIPERS CROFT
SPOONDELL
QUARRY WALK
BUTTERCUP CLOSE
LUTON-DUNSTABLE BUSWAY
8
12
24
43
32
35
42
40
10
15
23
34
4
22
19
28
26
45
46
20
18
27
48
25
47
31
37
44
50

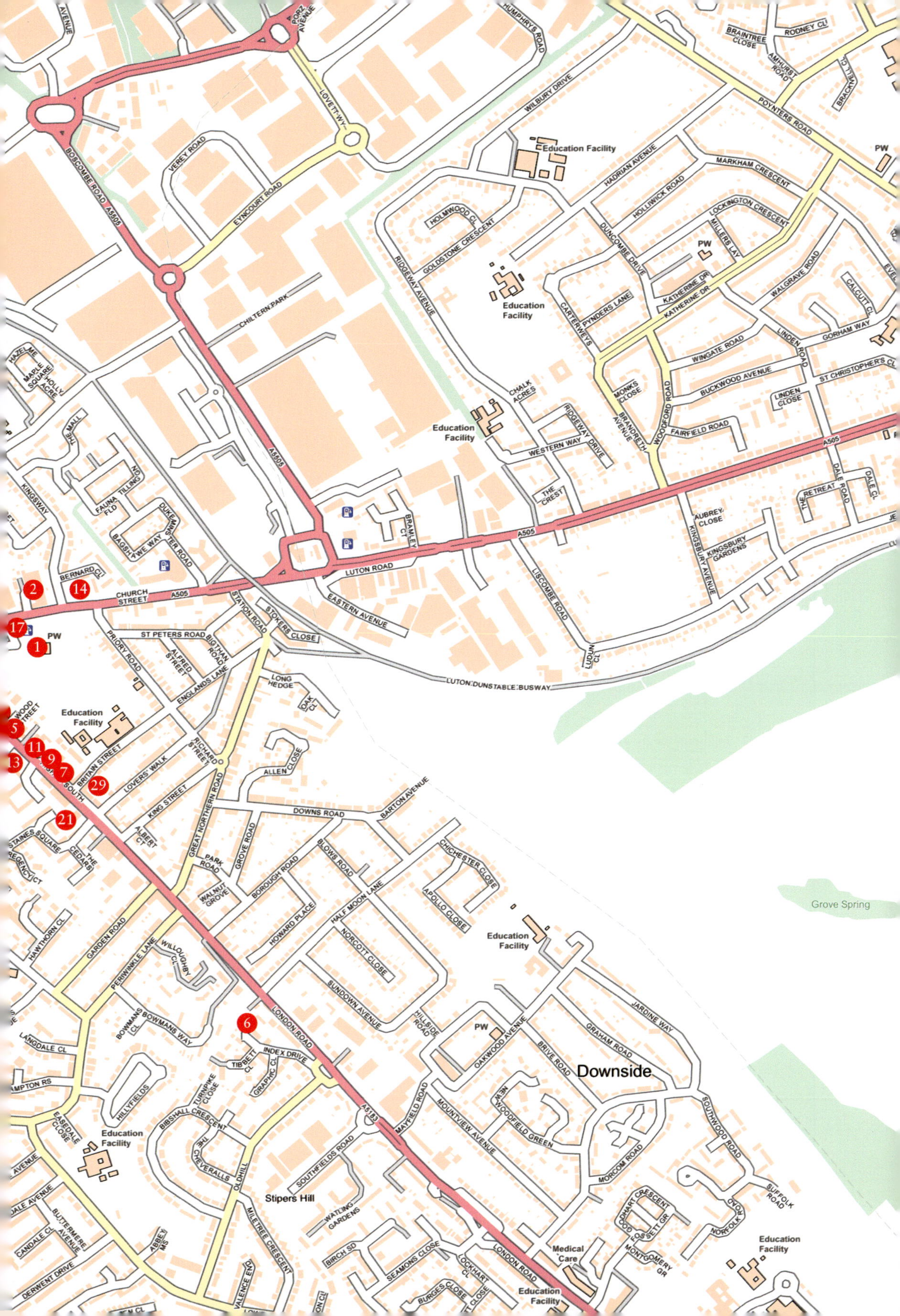

AVENUE
PORZ AVENUE
HUMPHRYS ROAD
BRAINTREE CLOSE
RODNEY CL
AMHURST ROAD
BRACKLEY CL
POYNTERS ROAD
LOVETT WY
WILBURY DRIVE
Education Facility
PW
BOSCOMBE ROAD A5505
VEREY ROAD
EYNCOURT ROAD
HADRIAN AVENUE
MARKHAM CRESCENT
HOLLIWICK ROAD
LOCKINGTON CRESCENT
HOLMWOOD CL
GOLDSTONE CRESCENT
DUNCOMBE DRIVE
MILLERS LAY
RIDGEWAY AVENUE
WALGRAVE ROAD
CALCUTT CL
KATHERINE DR
CARTERWEYS
PYNDERS LANE
Education Facility
CHILTERN PARK
GORHAM WAY
WINGATE ROAD
LINDEN ROAD
ST CHRISTOPHER'S CL
HAZEL MEAD
MAPLE SQUARE
HOLLY ACRE
MONKS CLOSE
BUCKWOOD AVENUE
CHALK ACRES
WOODFORD ROAD
LINDEN CLOSE
BRANDRETH AVENUE
FAIRFIELD ROAD
Education Facility
RIDGEWAY DRIVE
WESTERN WAY
A505
THE MALL
A5505
TILLING
FAUNA FLD
KINGSWAY
THE CREST
THE RETREAT
DALE ROAD
DALE CL
DUKE
SWINTER ROAD
BRAMLEY CT
AUBREY CLOSE
BAGSHAWE WAY
A505
KINGSBURY GARDENS
KINGSBURY AVENUE
LUTON ROAD
BERNARD CL
LISCOMBE ROAD
2
14
CHURCH STREET
A505
EASTERN AVENUE
STATION ROAD
STOKERS CLOSE
17
PW
1
ST PETERS ROAD
BIGTHAN ROAD
PRIORY ROAD
ALFRED STREET
LUDUN CL
LUTON DUNSTABLE BUSWAY
ENGLANDS LANE
LONG HEDGE
OAK CL
WOOD STREET
Education Facility
5
11
9
13
7
BRITAIN STREET
RICHARD STREET
ALLEN CLOSE
SOUTH
29
LOVERS' WALK
KING STREET
BARTON AVENUE
DOWNS ROAD
GREAT NORTHERN ROAD
21
ALBERT CT
STAINES SQUARE
REGENCY CT
CEDARS
THE
PARK ROAD
GROVE ROAD
BOROUGH ROAD
BLOWS ROAD
CHICHESTER CLOSE
WALNUT GROVE
HALF MOON LANE
APOLLO CLOSE
Grove Spring
HAWTHORN CL
GARDEN ROAD
HOWARD PLACE
NORCOTT CLOSE
Education Facility
PERIWINKLE LANE
WILLOUGHBY CL
SUNDOWN AVENUE
JARDINE WAY
BOWMANS CL
BOWMANS WAY
6
LONDON ROAD
HILLSIDE ROAD
PW
OAKWOOD AVENUE
GRAHAM ROAD
LANGDALE CL
TIBBETT CL
INDEX DRIVE
BRIVE ROAD
Downside
GRAPHIC CL
TURNPIKE CLOSE
HILLYFIELDS
MAYFIELD ROAD
NEW WOODFIELD GREEN
SOUTHWOOD ROAD
BIBSHALL CRESCENT
A5183
MOUNTVIEW AVENUE
EASEDALE CLOSE
Education Facility
THE CHEVERALLS
SOUTHFIELDS ROAD
MORCOM ROAD
SUFFOLK ROAD
AVENUE
OLDHILL
Stipers Hill
WATLING GARDENS
DALE AVENUE
BUTTERMERE AVENUE
MILETREE CRESCENT
NORFOLK ROAD
Education Facility
CANDALE CL
ABBEY MS
BIRCH SD
SEAMONS CLOSE
LOCKHART CL
LONDON ROAD
Medical Care
MONTGOMERY GR
DERWENT DRIVE
VALENCE END
BURGES CLOSE
Education Facility

Key

1. The Priory Church of St Peter
2. Old Palace Lodge
3. Priory House
4. The Old Anchor Archway, High Street North
5. The Saracen's Head
6. Former Half Moon Public House
7. The White Swan Public House
8. The Former Bull Public House, now No. 115 High Street North
9. Chew's House, High Street South
10. The Sugar Loaf Hotel, High Street North
11. Jane Cart Almshouses
12. Grove House
13. The Grey House, High Street South
14. Marshe Almshouses
15. No. 20 High Street North, now the Nationwide Building Society
16. The Friars, High Street South
17. Priory Church Hall
18. The Victoria Public House, West Street
19. The Former Borough Arms, Albion Street
20. West Street Mill
21. Former Carpenter's Arms, High Street South
22. Congregational Chapel, Edward Street
23. The Former Dunstable Borough Gazette Office
24. The Former Dunstable Grammar School
25. The Former Police Station, Icknield Street
26. Polish Catholic Church, Victoria Street
27. Strict Baptist Chapel, St Mary's Gate
28. The Former Baptist Chapel, West Street
29. The Little Theatre, High Street South
30. No. 52 High Street South, Former Hat Factory Manager's House
31. Dunstable Cemetery
32. The Globe Public House
33. Former Book Castle, Church Street
34. The Crown Inn
35. Chiltern House, High Street North
36. The Albion Buildings
37. The Former Wesleyan Chapel, High Street North
38. Methodist Church, the Square
39. Lloyds Bank, High Street North
40. The Former Post Office, DHSS Offices and Telephone Exchange
41. Petropolis House
42. The Former Union Social Club and Cinema
43. Old Fire Station, High Street North
44. The Former Chiltern Road School
45. St Mary's Roman Catholic Church, West Street
46. Quadrant Shopping Centre and Middle Row
47. Frances Ashton Almshouses
48. Salvation Army Dunstable Corps
49. The Grove Theatre/BBC Three Counties/Central Bedfordshire College
50. Incuba Centre

Introduction

The town of Dunstable was historically focused upon the intersection of two ancient routes: Icknield Way, running from east to west, and the Roman Watling Street, running from north to south. The crossroad remains a dominant feature in the topography of the town to this day. Dunstable has Roman origins. It was known as Durocobrivis and was centred on the crossroads, which appears to have been abandoned at the end of the Roman period.

The town was later re-established in the early twelfth century by Henry I, centred on the royal lodge of Kingsbury and the Augustinian priory, which was founded in 1131 but later dissolved in 1540. A market was established in the wide streets and marketplace, where permanent buildings began to encroach to form Middle Row, possibly from the early thirteenth century onwards.

The town continued to prosper as a market town in the post-medieval period and also as a significant staging post for coaches travelling along Watling Street. The nineteenth century saw the arrival of the railway, many new municipal

The book celebrates many of the town's oldest and iconic buildings, such as the former Ashton Grammar School…

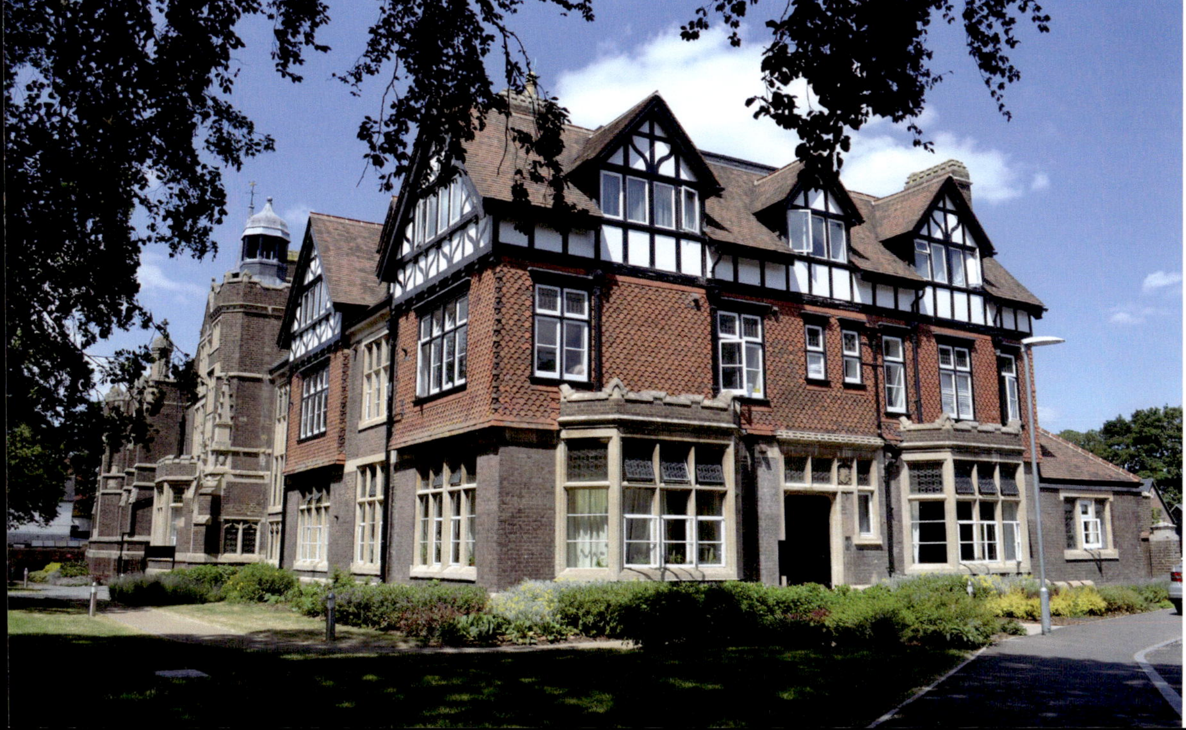

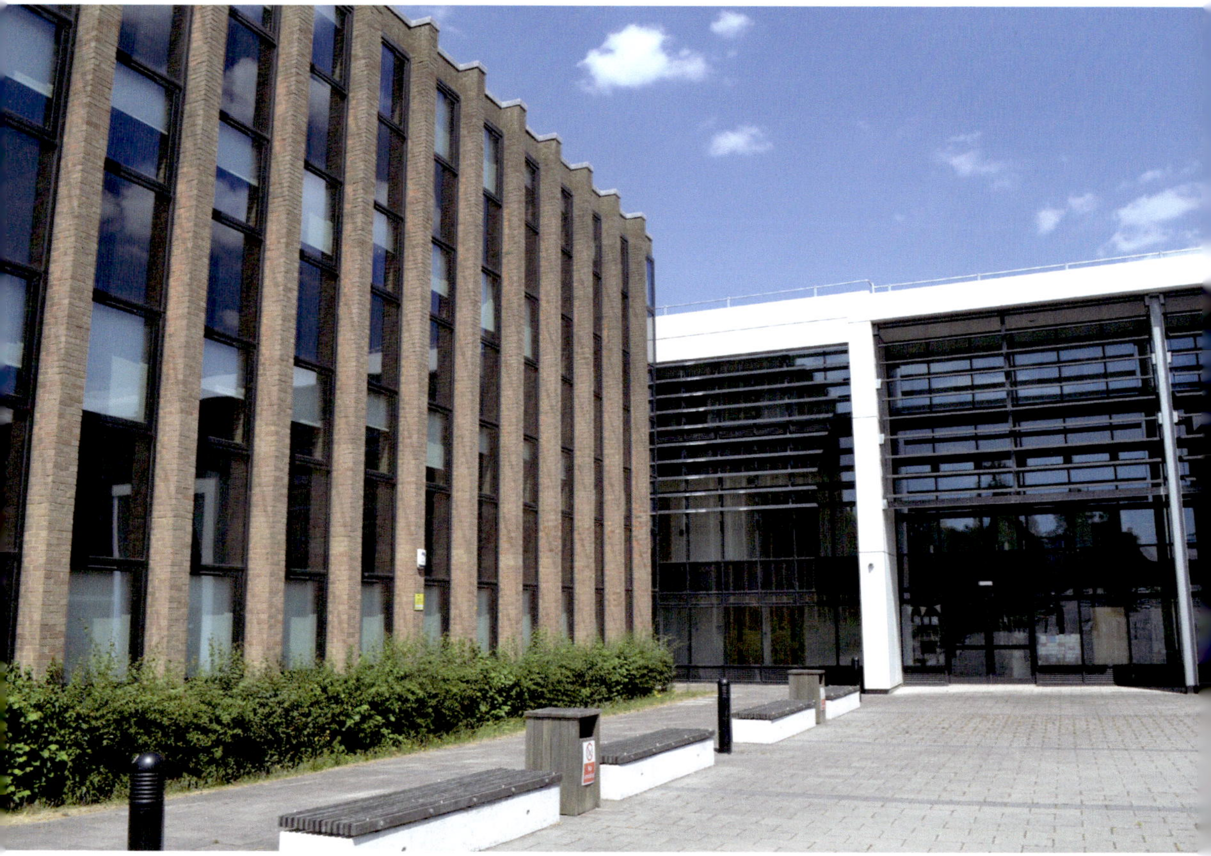

...right through to the modern age and the college complex.

buildings and the development of the backland with new terraced housing and small industrial premises – notably hat-making.

The twentieth century then subsequently saw the growth of the town as an engineering centre. Residential expansion continued apace, with associated provision for schools, churches and many other public buildings. Several of these buildings remain, shaping this town and making it what it is today, and they are the subject of this book. As with the many other books in the '50 Buildings' series I have written, especially Luton, Aylesbury and Watford, Dunstable often suffers from a negative perception and is portrayed unfairly in the media on far too many occasions. I hope, as always, that this book reminds many that Dunstable has much to offer and has played an important part in local, regional and national history. Such towns have a great deal to be proud of.

The 50 Buildings

1. The Priory Church of St Peter

Although many interesting historic events have taken place in the Augustinian priory of Dunstable and the subsequent Priory Church of St Peter, its importance lies in the reason why it was built and the purpose for which it has been, and continues to be, used.

The Priory of St Peter was founded by King Henry I. Henry had founded the town by at least 1109, and to safeguard its interests had built himself a house there called Kingsburie. Dunstable Priory was, initially, a daughter house of Holy Trinity, an Augustinian priory in Aldgate, London. The priory here was founded by 1125. There is evidence of a school in Dunstable as early as 1110 or 1115, which would eventually become part of the priory. The establishment of a priory of Augustinian black canons opposite his house completed the king's plans for the wellbeing of the town. Henry endowed the priory with the quarry at Totternhoe and the lordship of the town with all the privileges he had himself enjoyed when he held it in his own hands. The prior was thus the lord of the manor and responsible for collecting the taxes. These privileges were to be the cause of much trouble in later years and resulted in bitter quarrels between townsfolk and prior, although most of the money went to the exchequer to pay for the wars in France and Wales. Religious houses also had obligations to make regular and occasional payments to the pope in Rome.

The church was built in the form of a cross with a great tower at the crossing and with two smaller towers at the west end. Progress was slow and it was some seventy or eighty years before the church was complete. Work was impossible in the depths of winter, so progress was sporadic. The first prior of Dunstable, Bernard, was, with his brother Norman (afterwards prior of St Botolph, Colchester), closely associated with the introduction of the Augustinian order into England. The church and monastic buildings were erected under his rule and that of his two immediate successors, Prior Cuthbert and Prior Thomas. About this time, Alexander Nequam became master of the school. He was a great scholar and eventually became abbot of Cirencester. On 18 October 1213, Bishop Hugh II of Lincoln came to Dunstable and held a service of dedication. Lincoln was a huge diocese, stretching from the Humber almost to the Thames.

The fourth prior, Richard de Morins, elected 1202, was a man of considerable influence and ability. Richard ruled the priory for forty years and under him it entered upon the most prosperous period of its history. The priory attracted many pilgrims as they made their way to the shrine of Alban, to the south. King John gave permission for de Morins to move the bones of St Fremund from Cropredy in Oxfordshire to Dunstable. This vastly increased the number of pilgrims who came through the town, all of whom needed to be accommodated and fed. The priory was given farms, churches and granges as far away as the Peak District. The income from the huge flocks of sheep supported the priory in its work with the pilgrims and with the poor. The prior journeyed several times a year, inspecting his lands. In good seasons the farms brought the priory much wealth. In times of famine, they were a drain on the priory's resources.

The beautiful Norman church was not destined to remain complete for long. In June 1222, the roof of the presbytery fell, though a far greater disaster befell it in December of the same year when a violent storm that swept across the land brought down the two western towers. The fall of the northern tower ruined the west front; the southern one brought down the prior's house. The front was immediately rebuilt without towers. Its upper portion was designed with beautiful arcading and niches for statuary; the whole conception formed a lovely screen front with heavily buttressed turrets at the angles.

During the thirteenth and fourteenth centuries, Dunstable was the scene of many tournaments. Edward I attended those of 1279 and 1280, and Edward II in 1308. Edward III was here for the great tournaments of 1329 and 1341 with many of the nobility, and as a result the hospitality of the canons was strained to breaking point.

The last prior of Dunstable was Gervase Markham. He was elected in 1525. Within ten years dark clouds threatened the monastic horizon. Men's thoughts and outlook were changing, and a new spirit was abroad. The Middle Ages were passing, and the closure of monasteries and the reign of King Henry VIII were to have an impact.

In 1533, Archbishop Cranmer came to Dunstable with the bishops of Winchester, London, Bath and Lincoln to judge his royal master's 'grete and weightie cause' and annulled Henry VIII's marriage to Queen Catherine of Aragon. It was the final act in the shameful proceedings. Dunstable had been chosen as Catherine was then residing at Ampthill. The court was opened in the Lady Chapel of the Priory Church on 10 May, Prior Markham taking part in the proceedings. Catherine was cited but failed to appear. On 23 May 1533, Cranmer declared the annulment of the king's marriage. He was now free to marry Anne Boleyn. This was the beginning of the break with Rome; the pope's authority had been publicly flouted.

The Dissolution of the Monasteries is well documented elsewhere. Henry VIII initiated the Valor Ecclesiasticus, a survey of the income of each religious house.

The smaller monasteries were dissolved by Act of Parliament in 1536. Pressure was then brought to bear upon the larger houses and the process went on until, by the spring of 1540, not one of the English monasteries remained. Dunstable Priory was never a wealthy house. Its income was not great, the revenues being estimated at but £334 13*s* 4*d* per year. The deed of surrender was signed on 31 December 1539, and the monastery dissolved in January 1540, the prior and the twelve canons all being granted pensions. Dispensations were granted to them to serve as secular priests.

The great church and the buildings of the monastery were kept standing intact for some few years since, in the scheme for the creation of new bishoprics, it was intended to create a see at Dunstable, with the priory church as its cathedral. Sadly, however, this beautiful church (with the exception of the parochial nave) shared the fate of the monastic buildings, being plundered of all that was valuable and left a ruin to become a quarry for the whole neighbourhood.

Prior Markham lived on through the changes of Edward VI's reign, and the reversions of that of Mary, until the dawn of the reign of Elizabeth, dying at Dunstable in 1561. He accepted no appointment and lived quietly in the

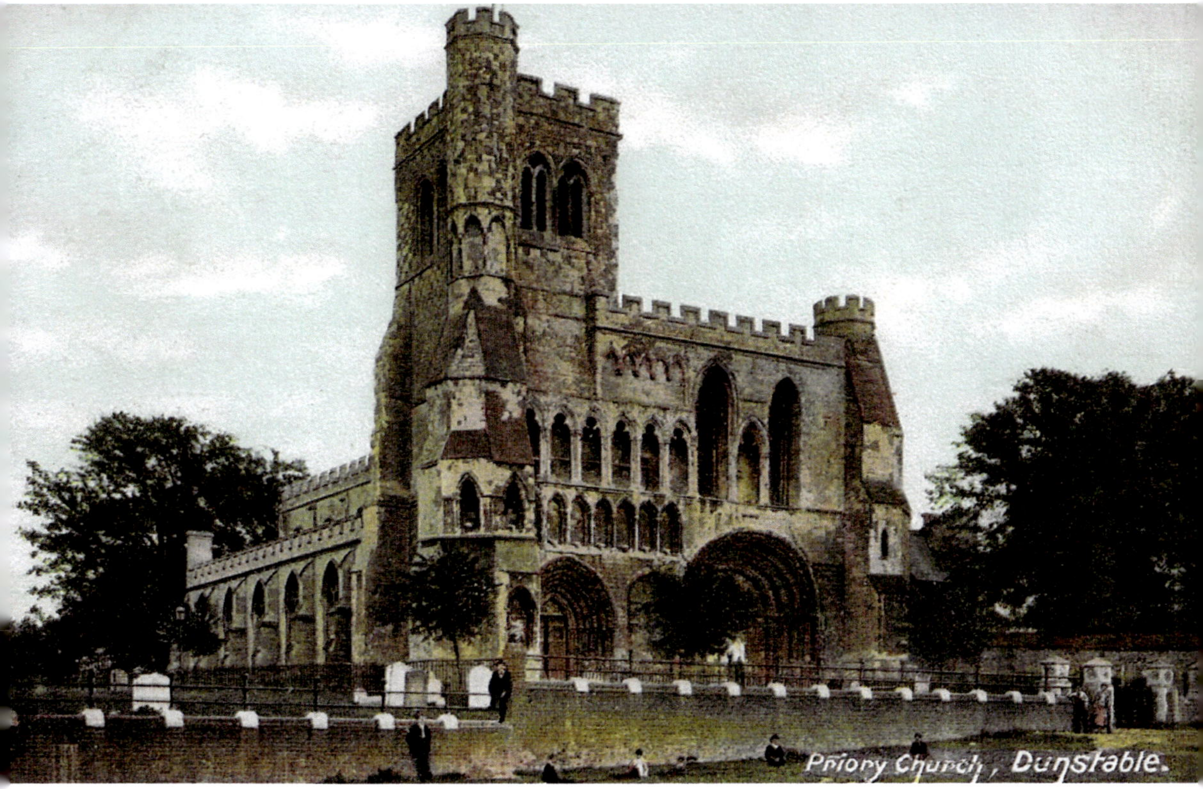

Priory Church in Edwardian times.

town on his considerable pension. He had a housekeeper, a manservant and a maidservant. At his death he still possessed his chalice, vestments and 'ornaments and implements for a chapel' and in his will he left them to his cousin to keep in case 'they may at any time hereafter be occupied in the church again'. He was buried in the church on 23 September.

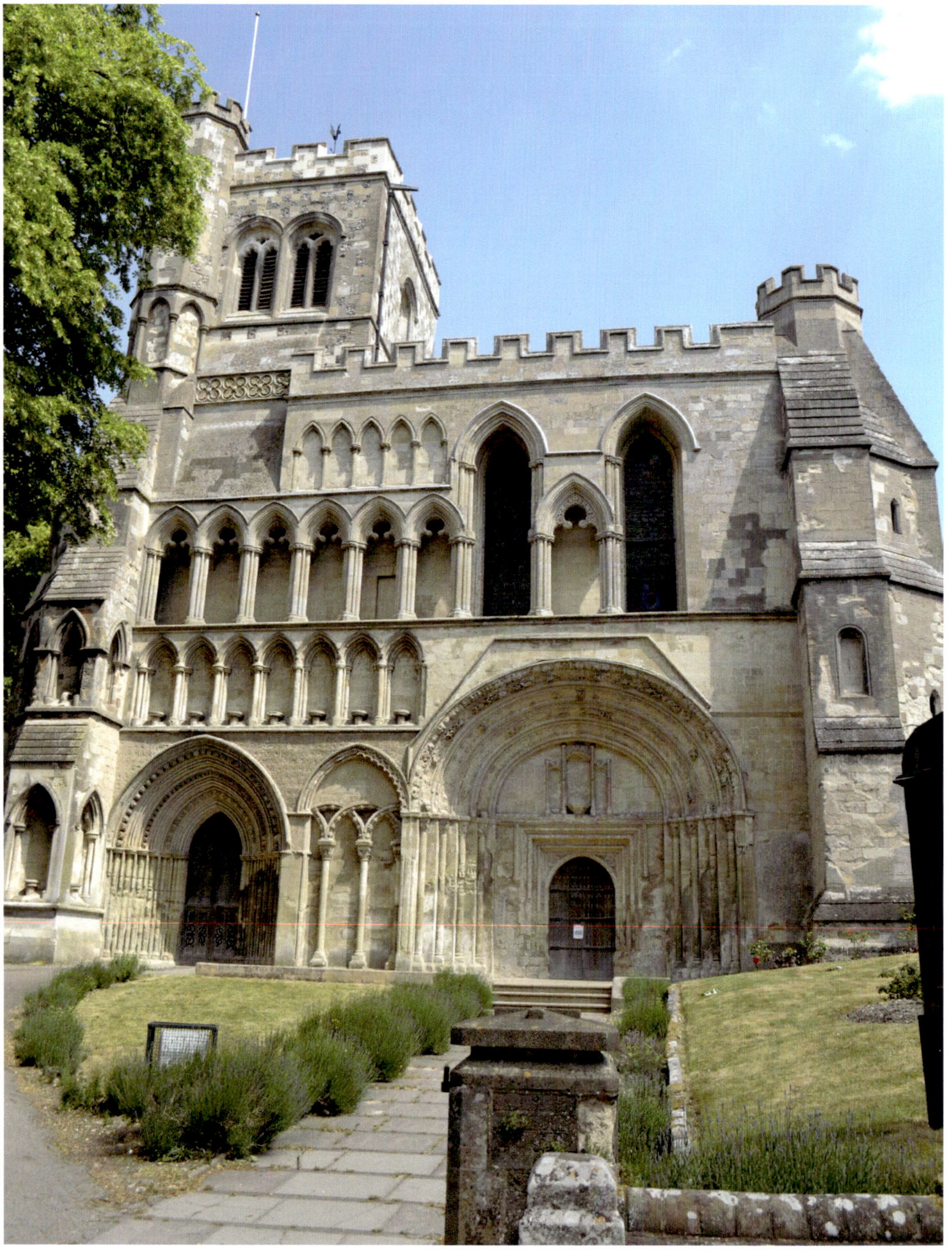

'Confusing and confused', as described by Pevsner.

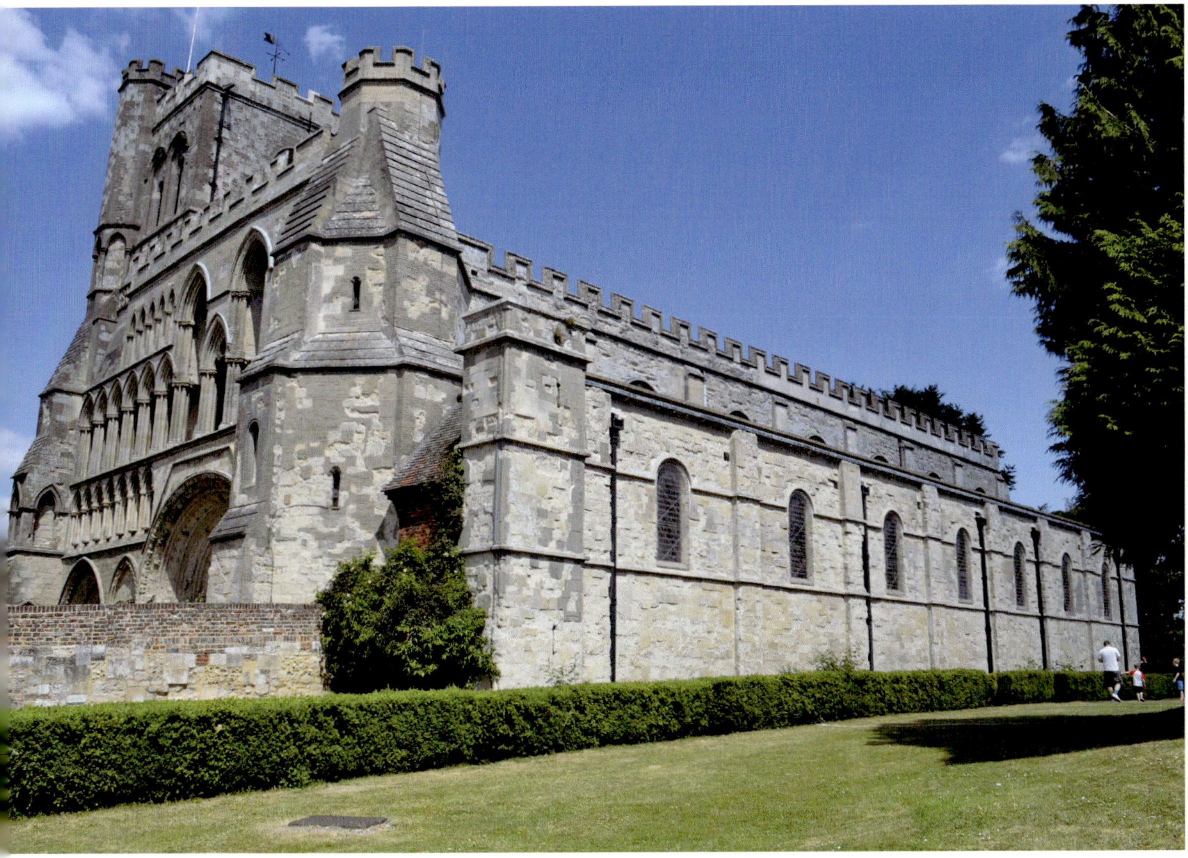

One of the most important buildings in the region.

Today, Priory Church remains a great historic monument and has played an important role in not only the history of the town, but that of the country. This Norman building is incredible, despite being a mere remnant of its former glory. Indeed, Pevsner describes the west face of the building as 'both confusing and confused'. It has also been described as 'unique and interesting … with a certain enigmatic charm in its asymmetry'.

2. Old Palace Lodge

The Old Palace Lodge in Church Street, with the adjacent Kingsbury Court, was originally all one building known as Kingsbury, so called because a palace built by King Henry I once stood on or near the site. A popular hotel up until early 2023, it was opened by Creasey Hotels Ltd in 1960. Walter Creasey, licensee of the Halfway House from 1939, became mayor of Dunstable in 1965. The town's football ground at Brewers Hill is named Creasey Park in his memory.

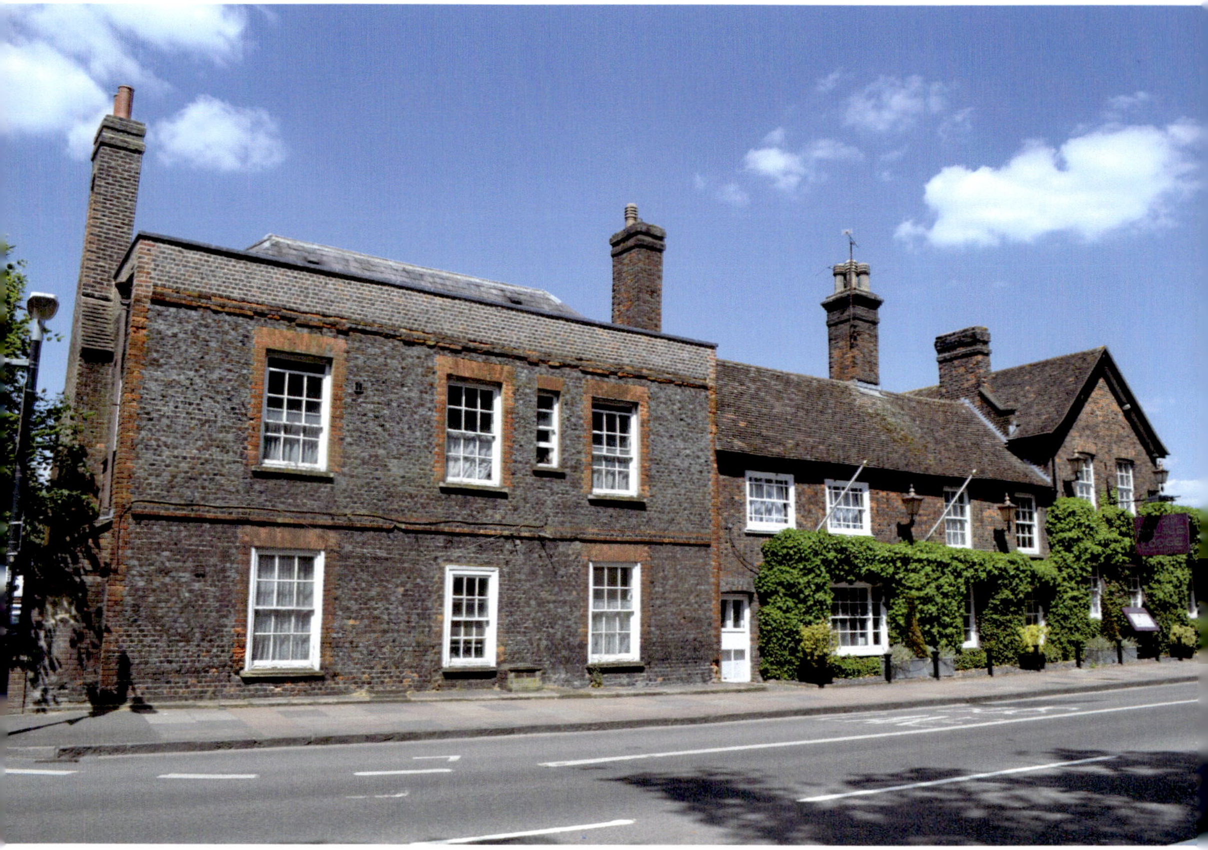

The Old Palace Lodge, now a hotel.

The history of this building, however, goes back many centuries. Henry I came to the throne in 1100 and for six years continued the violent quarrel previously waged between his eldest brother, Robert, and his deceased brother, William II. He captured Robert in 1106 and so became undisputed King of England and Duke of Normandy.

Wanting to develop national and international trade, he planted a business centre on Dunstable crossroads. To encourage this and to provide a royal presence, he had a palace built and installed a housekeeper (or steward). Kingsbury Palace was finished and furnished ready for a royal visit in 1109. From then on there were numerous royal visits, the most important being Henry's and Stephen's Christmas courts and the peace conference between King Stephen and the future King Henry II. When the building got older and more costly to maintain, King John gave it to Dunstable Priory, but there were later informal visits and in 1329 it hosted a royal tournament.

Just before the dissolution, Sir Thomas Wolsey's secretary, George Cavendish, bought it. In 1525, he was president of the prestigious Dunstable Fraternity.

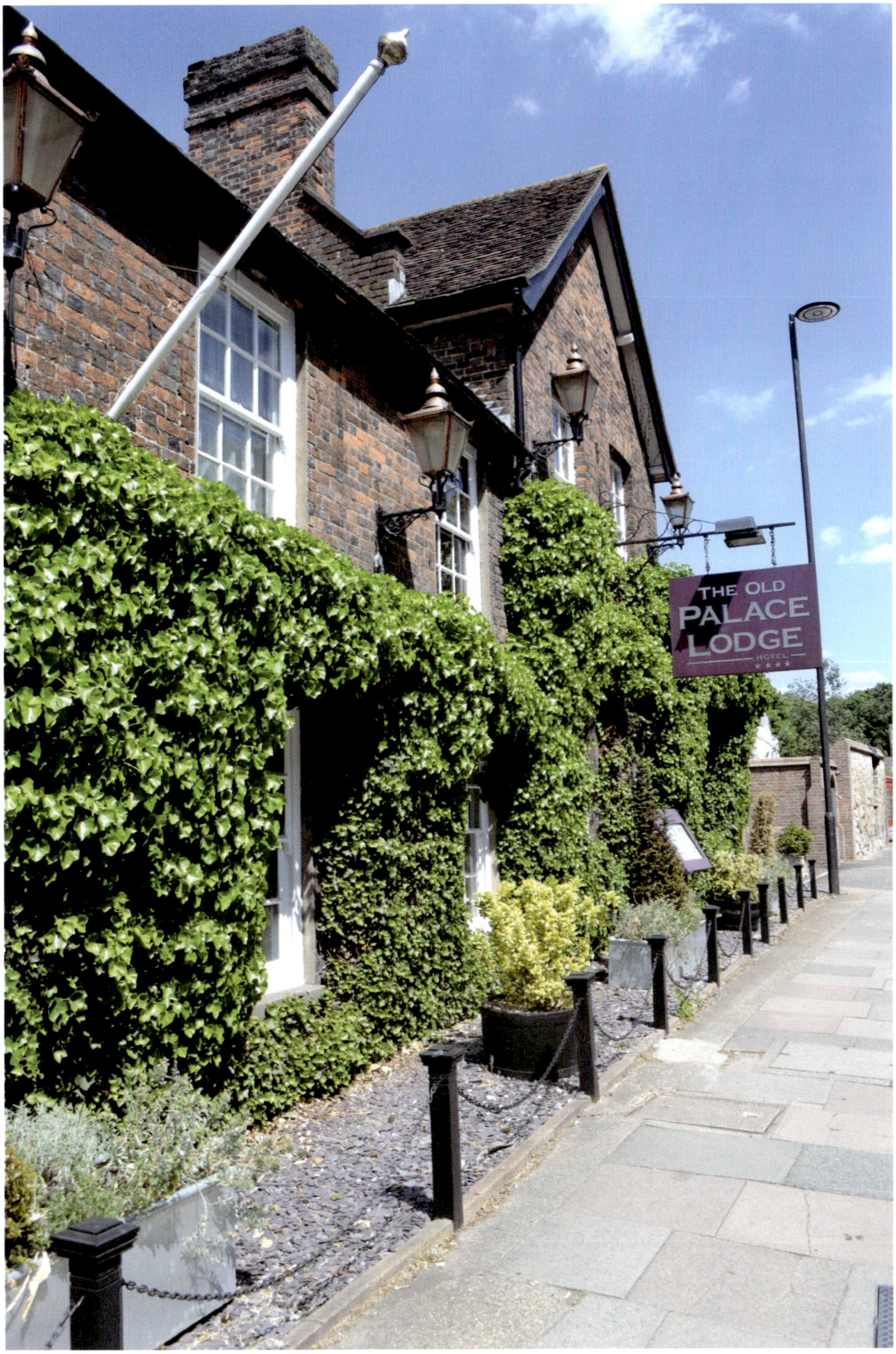

The Old Palace Lodge.

By 1600 William Marshe and his wife Elizabeth were living at Kingsbury, and their three surviving children grew up there. By the early nineteenth century the house belonged to Kingsbury Farm, which consisted of 164 acres scattered through the parishes of Dunstable, Houghton Regis and Caddington.

In the 1920s the eastern end of the house was re-roofed, with a gable end facing Church Street, which altered the appearance of the façade. In the 1930s the house was divided into two dwellings: one part being Dr Ashton's house, called Kingsbury Court, and the other occupied for some time by Mr Wallis, being renamed Old Palace Lodge. In 1959 this house was bought by Creasey Hotels and the following year, its refurbishment completed, it opened as the Old Palace Lodge Hotel.

In the same year a barn that formerly belonged to Kingsbury Farm, and was later Kingsbury Stables, was converted into the public house, becoming The Norman King. On the wall outside is the following inscription: 'On the site of this inn and the adjoining ground, Henry I had a palace built where he regularly stayed from 1109, and which was known as Kingsbury.' King Stephen entertained his nephew, the future King Henry II, at Kingsbury in 1153 when he made him his heir. In 1204 King John gave the palace to the priory and from then on the royal family stayed at the priory and his courtiers at the palace. When the present inn was built the local Totternhoe stone quarry had closed, so the stone was brought from a Norman castle and a cottage near Cambridge, with panelling from a medieval inn at Caxton in Cambridgeshire.

In early 2023 the hotel was suddenly closed to customers and used to house asylum seekers by the government's Home Office, a decision that was controversially received with such headlines as 'Old Palace Lodge: Row continues over Dunstable hotel's Home Office contract to house asylum seekers – A motion asking for Dunstable Town Council to contact hotels to reject block bookings for all their rooms was rejected'.

3. Priory House

This beautiful Grade II* listed building, Priory House, is one of the most significant buildings in Dunstable and remains popular with visitors and residents to this day. The distant view of the Priory Church is possible because the Munt and Brown hat factory, which stood over what is now the entrance to Priory Gardens, was demolished in 1909. The manager of the factory had previously lived in Priory House, which stands on the site of the original hospice, where canons from the priory monastery would attend to the needs of travellers passing through the town. The medieval vaultings from that time can still be seen within the building.

From 1545, with the Dissolution of the Monasteries, the building became a private house. One of the earliest owners was the Crawley family who later owned Stockwood Park in Luton and who used part of the building as an early hospital

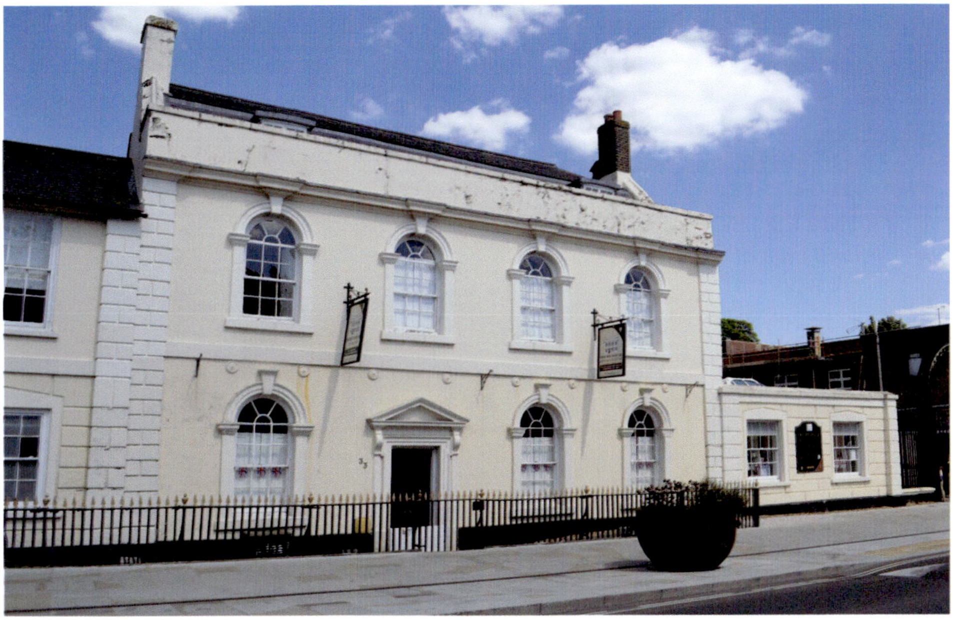

Above: Priory House on High Street South.

Right: Priory House, now a heritage centre for the town.

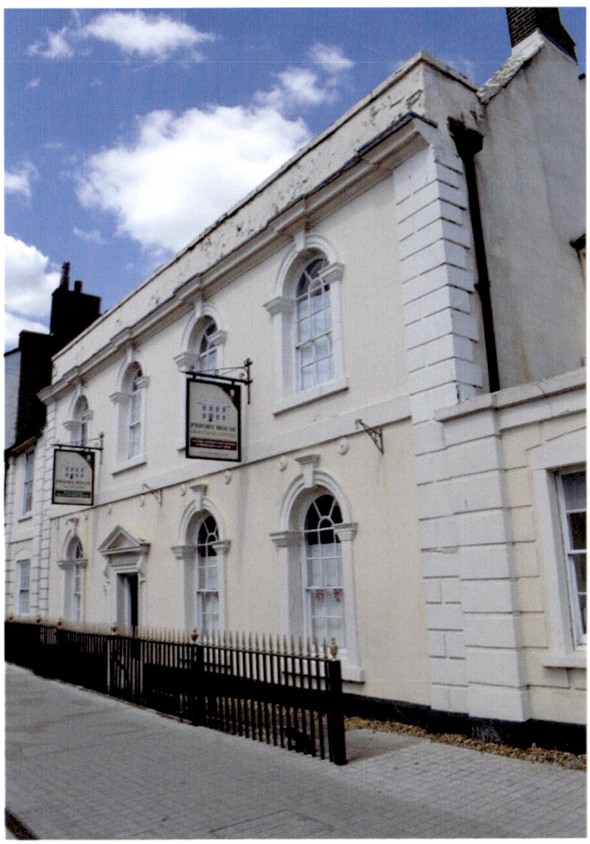

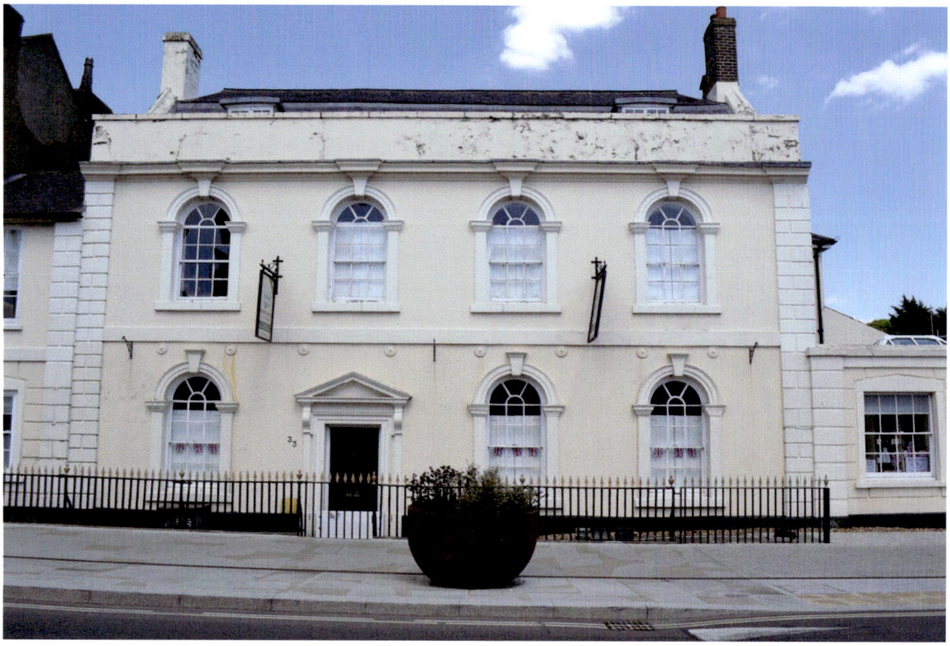

Above: The impressive frontage of Priory House.

Below: Priory House from Priory Gardens.

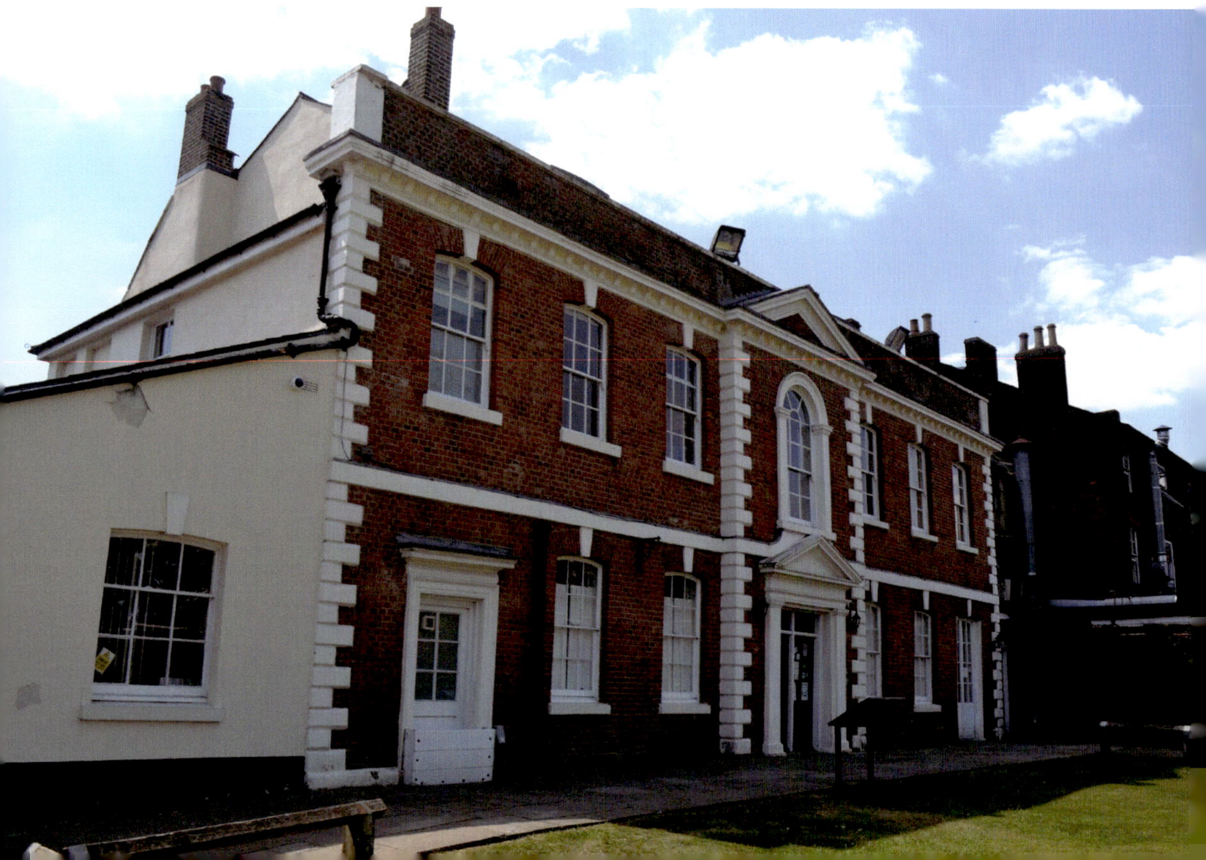

for the mentally ill. In 1743 the original stone-vaulted hall was incorporated into a much larger house with the Georgian façade and internal details we see today. By the nineteenth century Priory House was owned by the Munt family, who built a hat factory next to it on the site of the present gateway from High Street South, though the factory was eventually demolished.

Since 1956 the building was initially occupied as offices, firstly by Dunstable Borough Council and South Bedfordshire District Council and, more recently, by a private company. With the aid of a Heritage Lottery Grant, Dunstable Town Council converted this magnificent piece of history and architecture into a Heritage and Tourist Information Centre in 2005.

The oldest part of Priory House is the magnificent vaulted undercroft. It is a typical two-storey Norman stone building of the late twelfth century of a type known as a 'hall and cellar house'. Although there are various theories about it, no record has been found as to who built it or why. It remains one of the finest buildings in the town.

4. The Old Anchor Archway, High Street North

This part of the High Street has changed considerably over the centuries, but one constant is the early seventeenth-century gatehouse, the now Grade II* listed Anchor archway. The original town hall stood between The Crown and the Anchor Gateway. The old town hall has long since gone.

In 1866 the Old Market House premises were bought from Queen Victoria by the new borough council (formed in 1864) for council meetings and for a police

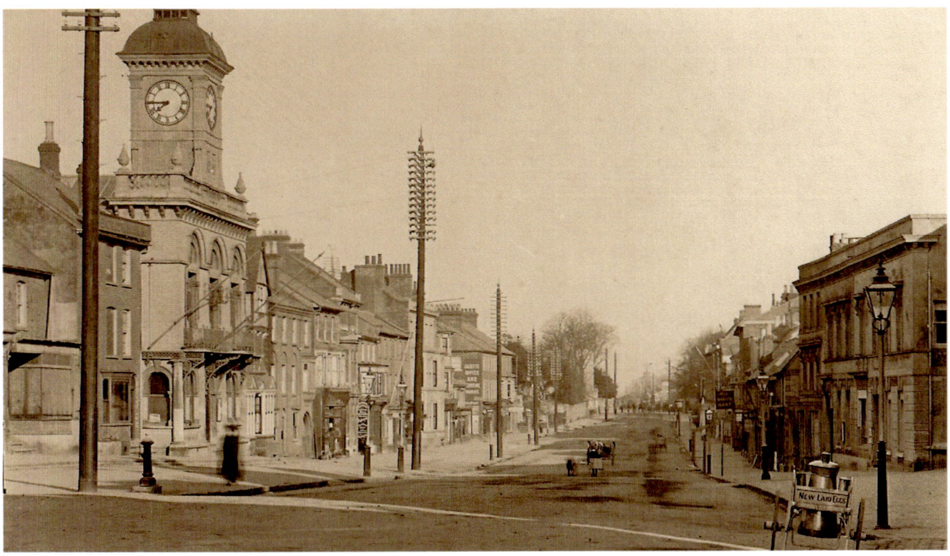

High Street North and the old town hall and corn exchange, visible with its clock tower.

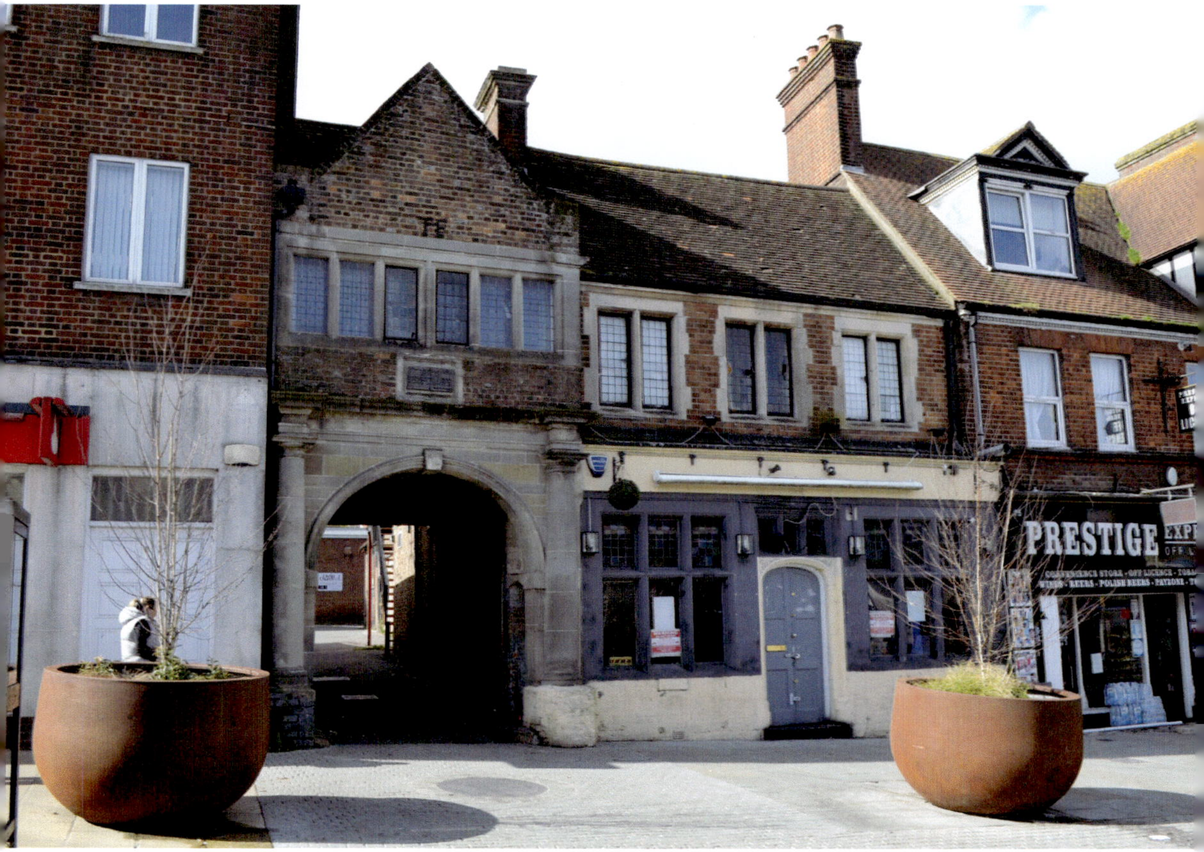

The archway today.

court. In 1869 a clock tower was erected and in 1872 a corn exchange and plait hall was fitted behind the town hall in the Anchor's yard. Fire engines were also accommodated in the yard, but rather unfortunately were unable to get out of it when the town hall burnt down in 1879.

A new town hall was built in 1880 and included municipal offices and a main hall for meetings and entertainments. A new clock tower was built and could be seen from a considerable distance. Sadly, the town hall was sold to the Pearl Assurance Co. Ltd in November 1965 and pulled down the following year, making way for the buildings we see today.

The Anchor Gateway was the stone gateway to a sixteenth-century inn called the White Horse, which no longer exists. The Anchor Inn was built on the site of the White Horse, and the gateway became known as the Anchor Archway. Henry VIII stayed at the White Horse in 1537 after he refused an invitation to stay at the nearby priory.

The name of the White Horse was transferred to a pub in Church Street, the Anchor, and was known as a poacher's tavern. A succession of landlords occupied the Anchor, but by 1894 the Anchor Inn had closed down and the premises were occupied by Middleton and Gutteridge solicitors. S. D. B. Middleton was 'solicitor and clerk to the Borough Magistrates, Steward of the Manor of Markyate Street, perpetual commissioner, solicitor to the local branch of Bassett and Co. Bank and to Dunstable and Markyate Street Building Societies'. Albert Gutteridge was 'solicitor and commissioner for oaths and certified bailiff under the Law of Distress Amendment Act'.

Despite such a fascinating history, the building has had successive uses, including a building society and post office, and became a public house once again with names such as The Bank and latterly Finbars White Horse. In 2023, it was once again closed and up for sale, its future uncertain.

5. The Saracen's Head

The Saracen's Head is Dunstable's oldest surviving inn and is located in High Street South. Parts of the building date back to the sixteenth century. It was possibly opened by the nearby priory as an extra lodging house for pilgrims.

In the sixteenth century, Adam Hilton of the Saracen's Head was the 'Local Receiver' or 'Bailiff', who collected the income from the local religious houses. By the seventeenth century, from about 1645, the increased traffic along Watling

The Saracen's Head.

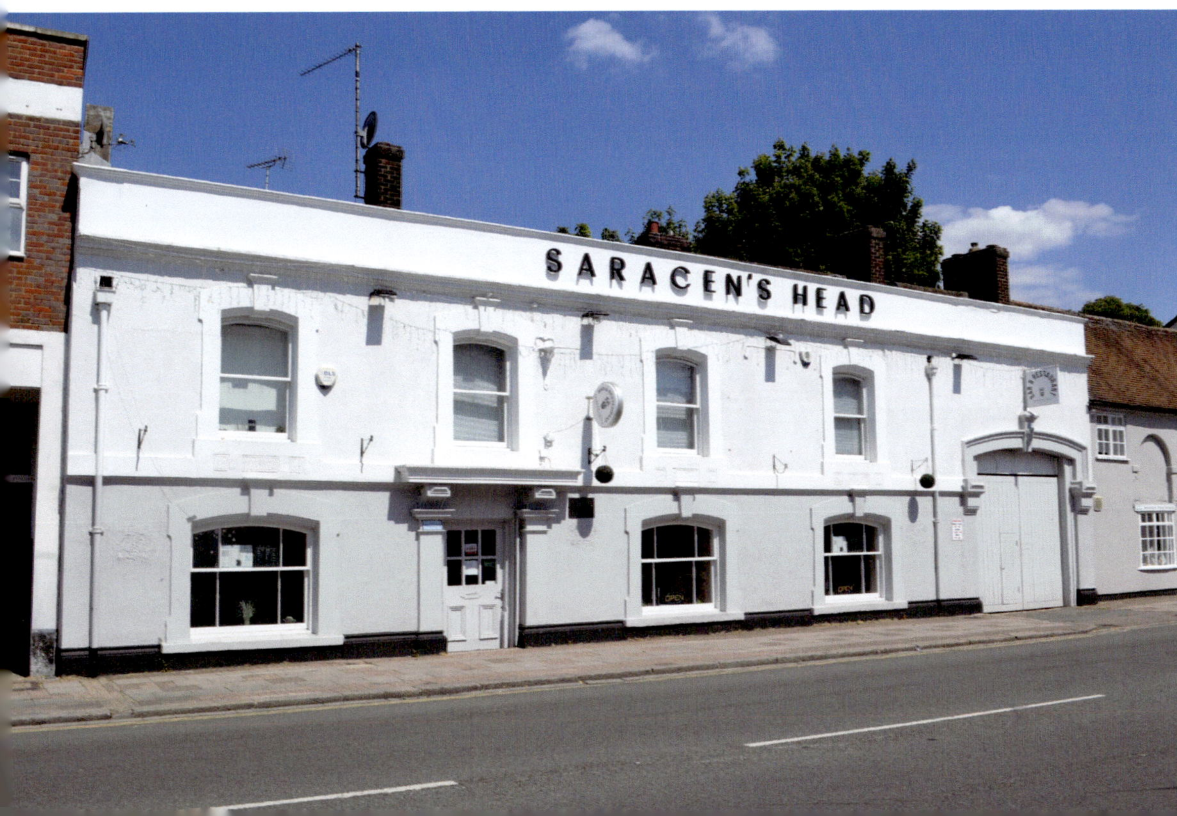

Street was benefitting the innkeepers, and the Saracen's Head extended to provide extra stabling and accommodation. In 1649 the Saracen's Head was mentioned in a deed as belonging to Francis Dingley.

Sadly, much of the old building was destroyed in a fire in 1815 and was rebuilt on its present street line. When it was being restored, a buried hoard of coins was discovered dating back to the Civil War. The landlord at the time had been a Roundhead and it is possible that he had hidden his savings when the town was raided by supporters of the king. The Cavaliers famously fired shots at the congregation in the Priory Church, and bullet holes can still be seen in the church door. Its unusually long frontage reflects its past life as not one but three inns: The George, The Saracen's Head and The Bell. Sadly, in 2023 it was no longer in business.

6. Former Half Moon Public House

The nearby village of Kensworth had two drinking establishments called The Half Moon. One was a public house, while the other was a beerhouse. At first glance it seems very strange to have two licensed premises of the same name in the same village, but they were a long way apart. The Half Moon beerhouse was in the village itself, whereas the Half Moon public house was at the extreme north-eastern tip of the parish – since boundary changes in 1985, it is now well inside Dunstable.

Kensworth was in Hertfordshire until 1897 when it transferred to Bedfordshire. The 1891 census reveals information about the licensee, Thomas Partridge, for over twenty years. At that date he was aged sixty-six. He had been born in Ivinghoe in Buckinghamshire. His wife, Martha, was a year younger than him and had been born in Tebworth.

The county-wide licence register of 1903 states that the owner of the establishment was Watford (Hertfordshire) brewer Benskin & Company Limited. The public house needed cleaning and sanitation was not satisfactory. It was 370 yards from the nearest licensed premises and had both a front door and a door from the yard at the side. The unsatisfactory sanitation may have had a hand in the closure of the premises ten years later.

In Volume II of *The Bedfordshire Magazine* in 1950/51, there is a distinctly colourful account of the pub:

> South of the town stood a toll-gate. Coaches could not avoid it but market goers and drovers escaped the toll by leaving the Watling Street bear the Pack Horse, following the old Drover's Way, and rejoining the main road by the Half Moon, doubtless spending their resultant saving at the small tavern on the high bank. To-day, half Moon Dairy is all that is left of this once colourful tavern. It was the first call from the south for packhorse drivers, London journeymen and pedlars.

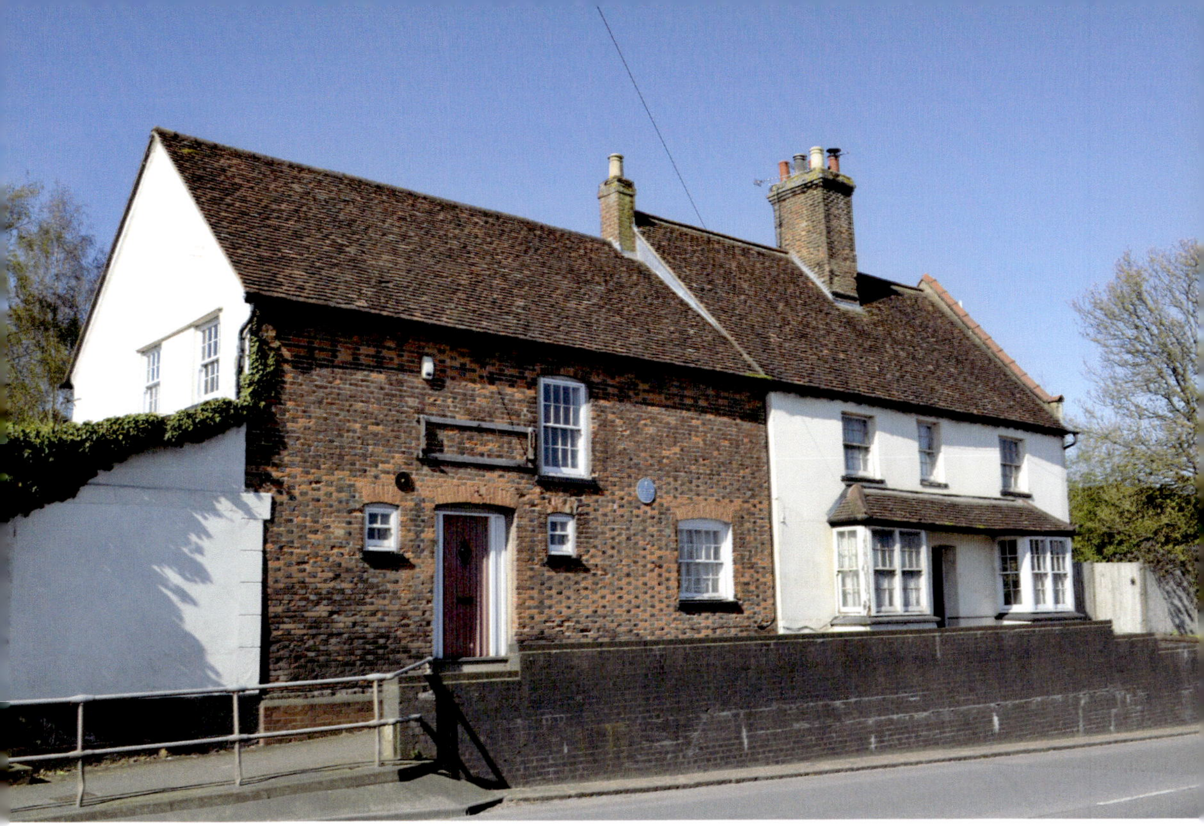

The former Half Moon public house.

> Local lore says that the highwaymen who picketed the road made it their headquarters. Authority Worthington Smith conjures up a picture of even earlier days. Behind the Half Moon, he cites the bull-baiting ring of Stuart times, when rich and poor alike goaded the unfortunate animal with knives, sticks and whips until it bled to death; this treatment was supposed to make the flesh more tender.

The Half Moon was listed in March 1976. It dates from the seventeenth century or earlier – 'altered but retaining a largely complete timber frame'. This noted pub had closed in 1914 and now has a blue plaque, which reads 'Former Half Moon Inn. Hostelry since 1750 and reputed haunt of highwaymen'. It is also said to be haunted by Dick Turpin. Today it is a private dwelling.

7. The White Swan Public House

The White Swan, located on High Street South, is one of the town's oldest pubs, dating from the seventeenth century. There is certainly evidence that a building existed here in the sixteenth century, though, with remnants of timber framing inside. A pub called The Falcon was recorded in 1542, which may have been located here. In the seventeenth century, the inn was owned by the Fossey family, who were well known locally, having their own pew in Priory Church. At that

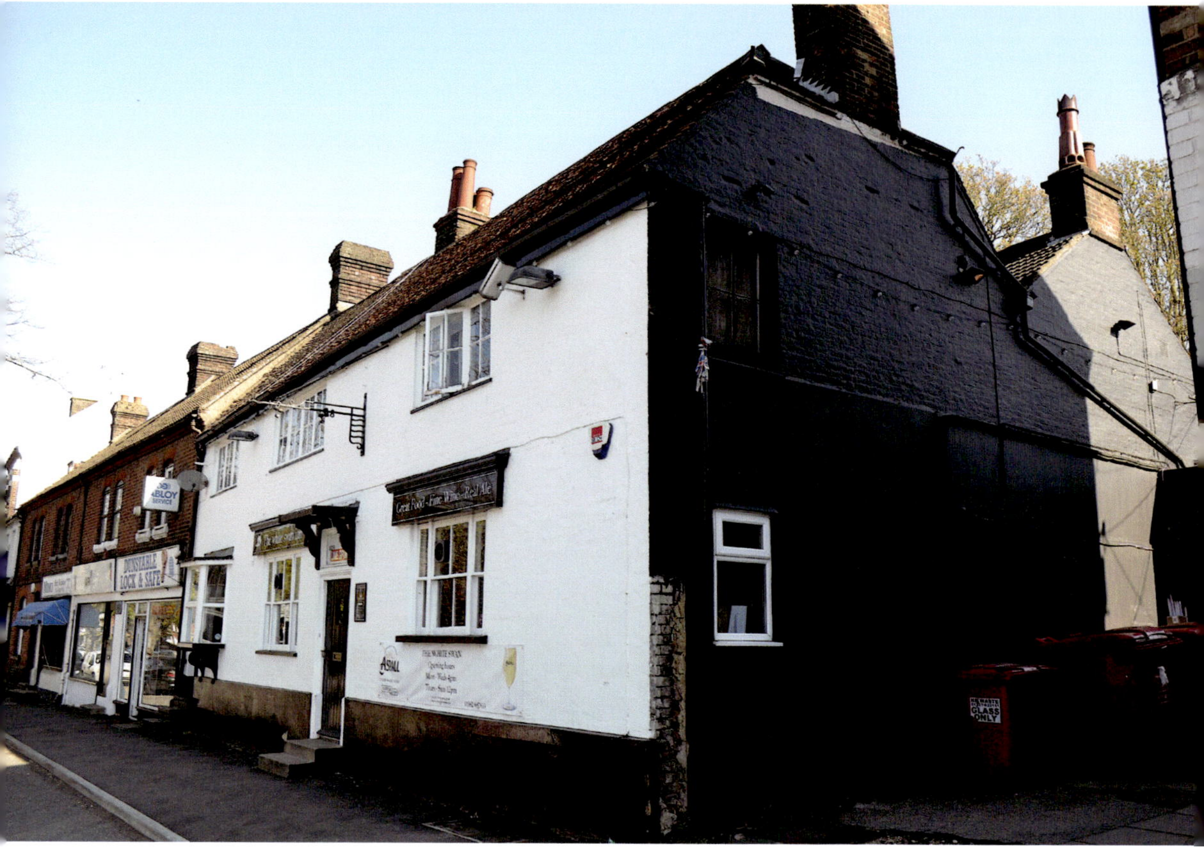

The White Swan public house.

time it was known as The Two Black Boys, but it was called The Swan by the second half of the eighteenth century. By the nineteenth century, the inn had been taken over by the Gilberts, also well known locally.

8. The Former Bull Public House, now No. 115 High Street North

On the corner of High Street North and Union Street, this building was once the Prince's Arms, then the Red Hart and, for a short time, the Rose and Crown before becoming the Bull or the Black Bull in the eighteenth century. The large coaching yard was to the rear.

A deed dated 4 July 1649 refers to 'the Prince's Arms, now the Red Hart in the North end and North St. of Dunstable'. Another deed, dated 16 October 1663, refers to 'the Red Hart Inn in North St Dunstable occupied by William Neale' being conveyed to William Ketteridge, innholder of Dunstable. It also mentions '15.5 acres of land in Dunstable and Houghton Regis' which is bounded by

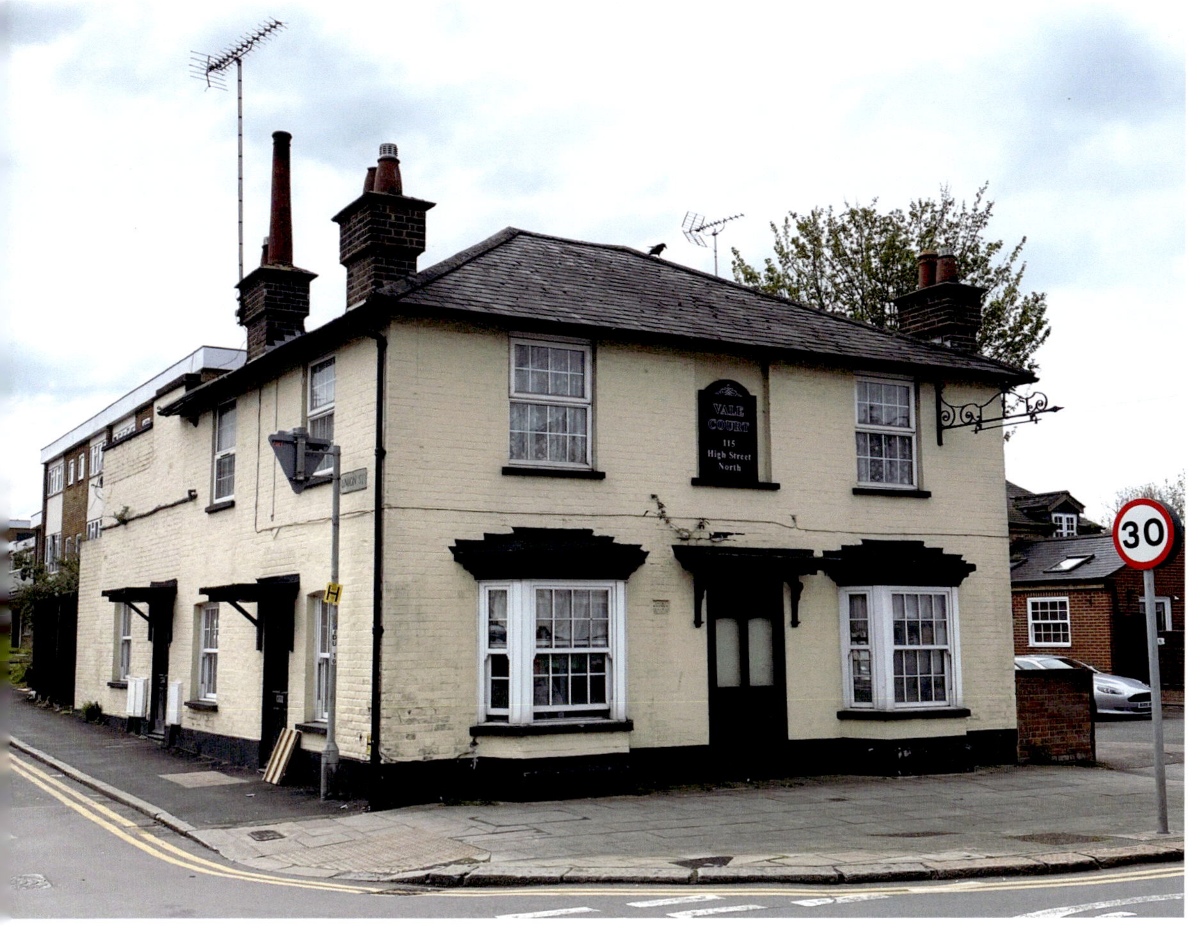

Daily passed by many, this building was once a public house. It had many names, but its last was The Bull.

'Deadman's Hill' and 'Leighton Gap' and the 'Icknield Way'. In 1679 the inn was transferred from William Ketteridge to Henry Earle, a coachman from London. By 1690 the inn was known as the Black Bull. Throughout the eighteenth century it had a number of owners, eventually becoming known as the Bull with successive owners until the 1950s. Like many inns of the town it has since been converted for residential use, but certainly still has the appearance of an inn.

9. Chew's House, High Street South

Another remarkable building on High Street South is Chew's House. This building, now used as church offices, was originally a charity school. The additional school buildings on the right later became the town library before being converted into

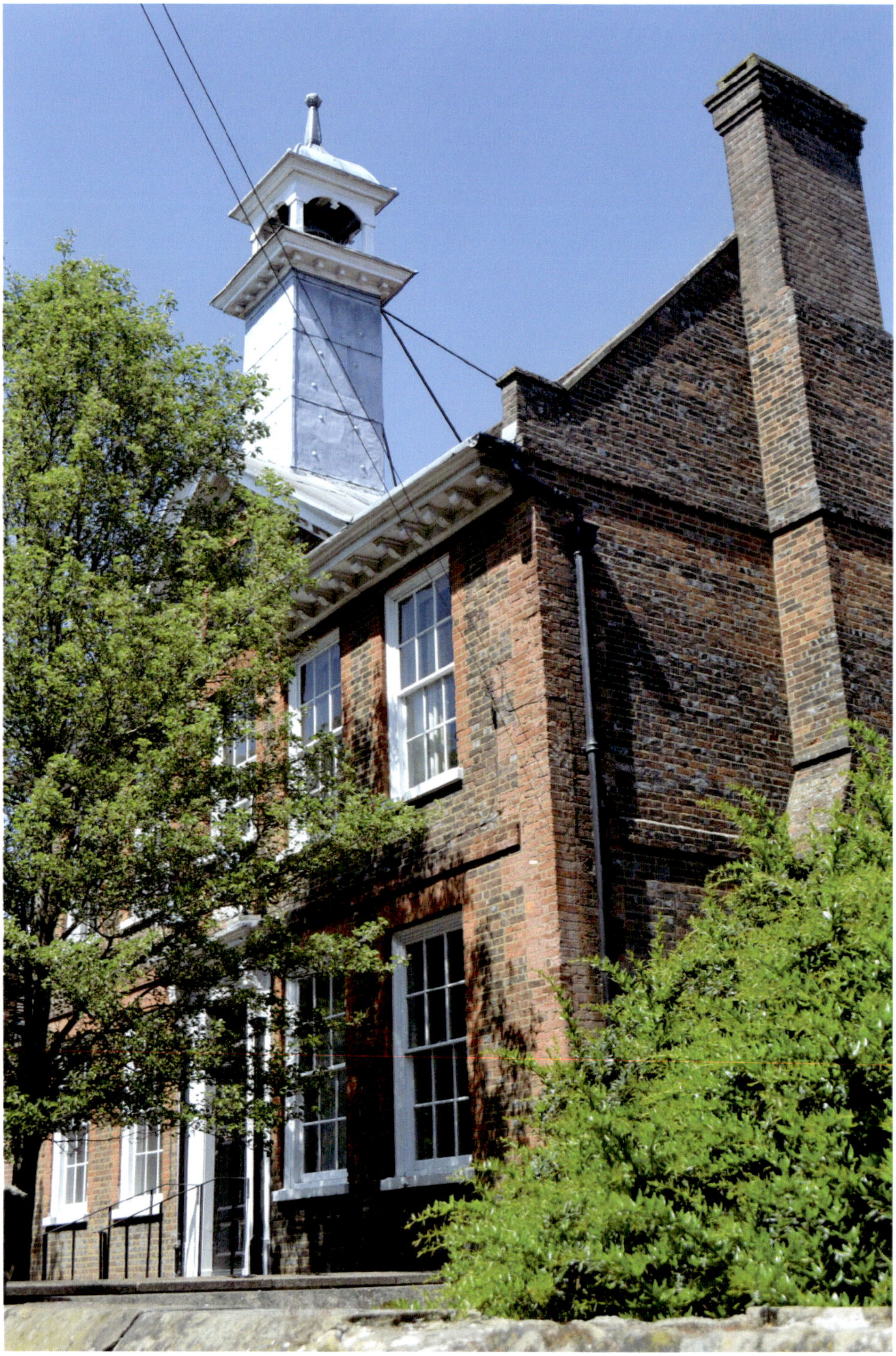

Chew's House. The school closed in 1905.

a theatre by Dunstable Repertory Company. William Chew, who died in 1712, intended to provide a school for forty poor boys of Dunstable but died before doing so. He left money to his two surviving sisters, Jane Cart and Frances Ashton, and to Thomas Aynscombe, the eldest son of another sister. They saw that his wishes were carried out and the school was built in 1715.

At the very fine front entrance to the building is a stone that commemorates the founding of the school by Mrs Frances Ashton, Mrs Jane Cart and Mr Thomas Aynscombe. The unusual figures are of boys wearing the uniform of the old school with one of the uniformed scholars doffing his cap. Photographs of the figures were used to create the present facsimiles of the originals after these were stolen. Despite a large reward, the thieves were never caught.

William Chew died in 1712 without a wife or children and without leaving a will. However, he had taken considerable interest in the plight of poor boys

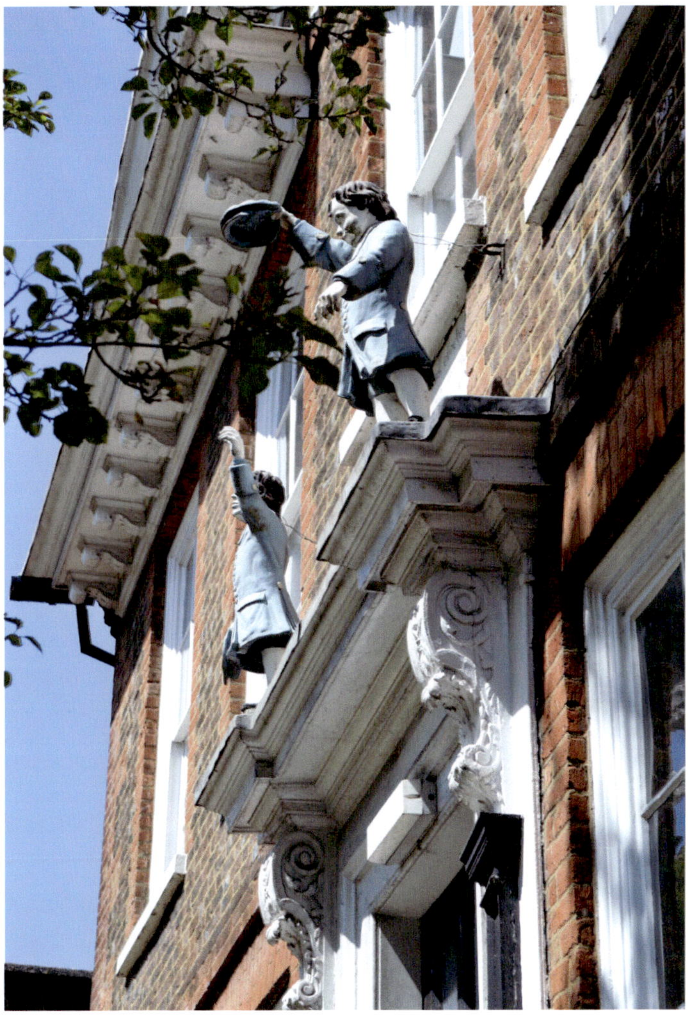

The boys wearing the uniform of the old school above the main door.

and had for many years provided clothing for them. He had also expressed the intention of establishing a free school in Dunstable. Consequently, his estate of about £28,000 passed to his remaining family. It was they who arranged for the schoolhouse to be built in his name.

The school had strict rules as to who was eligible to attend. The founders were especially concerned that the school should be closely connected with the Church of England. To be eligible as a pupil, a boy had to be over seven years old, born in wedlock and be able to read from the New Testament, plus his parents must have regularly attended services at their parish church for at least two years prior to application. Only one boy from a family could attend the school at any one time and each boy had to leave at the age of fourteen. At first, the boys were not expected to take time off for holidays, apart from two weeks at harvest time to help in the fields. Later, in 1791, the trustees allowed the boys to have four weeks at harvest time and one week at Easter and Whitsun.

During the second half of the eighteenth century the trustees found it difficult to pay the running costs, but the school managed to continue and was able to supply free clothing until 1888. Sadly though, in 1905, the school closed completely and the governors decided that the charity funds should be used for local scholarships and apprenticeships. The building was eventually used by several clubs and societies.

10. The Sugar Loaf Hotel, High Street North

The Sugar Loaf Hotel on High Street North is one of the town's most distinctive buildings and can be recognised in hundreds of old High Street photographs. It was built in around 1717 and became a fashionable stopping place for horse-drawn carriages travelling along Watling Street. In the coaching era's heyday, the Sugar Loaf kept a magnificent stable of greys, 'admired by all the nobility'.

It was soon after the Civil War that private travellers began to expect, and demand, a higher standard of accommodation. As such, the local entrepreneur George Briggs built and then modernised the building to cater for such clientele, refusing all but the higher class of traveller. This included Queen Victoria and Prince Albert, who stopped here in 1841 and viewed a display of locally made straw plait. Lord Byron was another visitor and Daniel Defoe made it the venue for a scene in *Moll Flanders*. The hotel had a famous recipe for serving a local delicacy: Dunstable larks, netted in their thousands on Dunstable Downs.

Next door to the hotel is a fashion shop, which once occupied what was once the Sugar Loaf Tap. This was provided in 1861 as an extension to the exclusive and popular hotel next door when its owners were required to provide billets for soldiers. Guests had been required to make room for military men, who paid nothing for their beds, at great loss to the inn. The Sugar Loaf Tap was called the Soldiers House when it first opened.

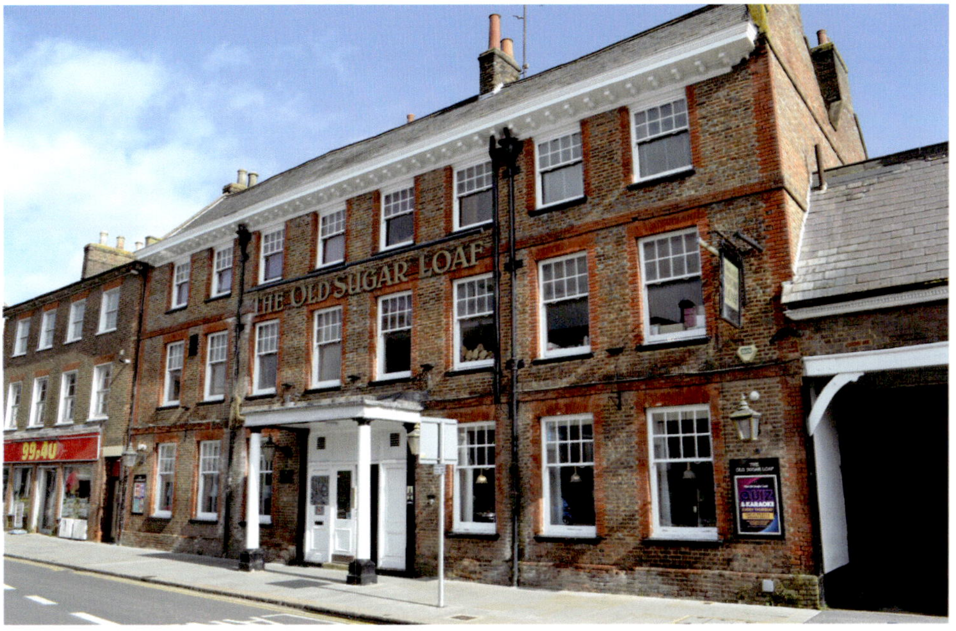

The Old Sugar Loaf, once visited by royalty during Victorian times.

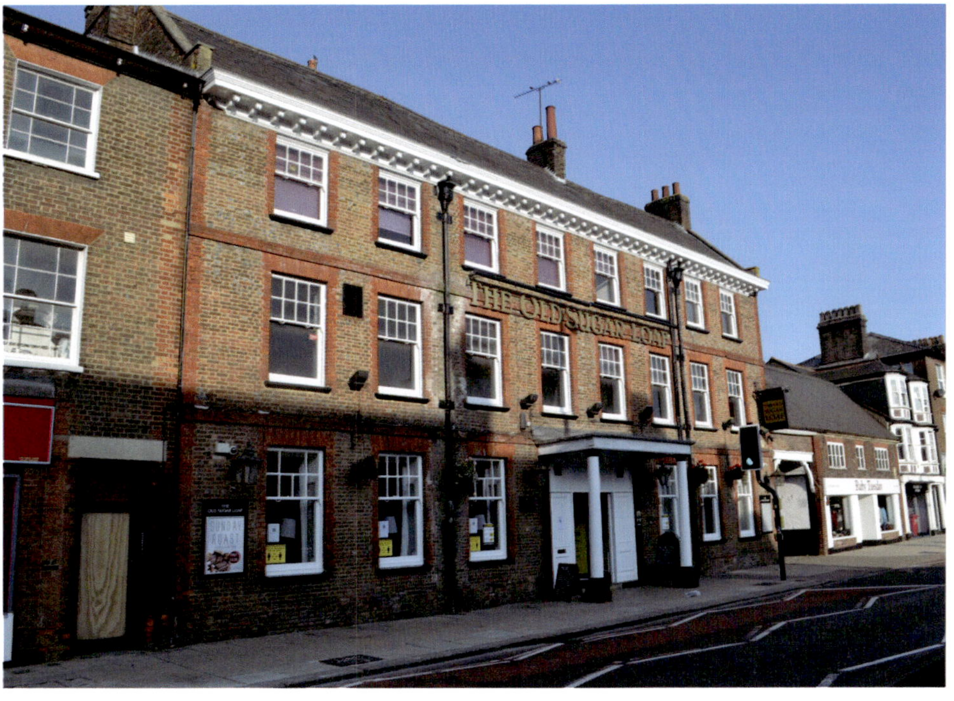

The Sugar Loaf Tap to the right of the building, once a billet for soldiers.

11. Jane Cart Almshouses

Set back off High Street South are the very fine Jane Cart Almshouses. These were provided by Mrs Jane Cart (1653–1736) to house six poor women, widows or spinsters who were members of the Church of England. One of Jane's sons, Thomas, had died in 1722 aged twenty-seven and the almshouses may have been intended as a memorial to him. Mrs Cart's other gifts to the town included the clock in the Priory Church tower and a huge painting for the church by Sir James Thornhill, which was allowed to disintegrate after it was damaged by rainwater in Victorian times. The considerable amount of property owned by Mrs Cart also included the Sugar Loaf Hotel on the High Street.

Jane was the youngest daughter of Thomas Chew, who was a haberdasher in Dunstable. She inherited No. 10 High Street North from her mother, so this may have been the family home and business. She married James Cart, a merchant and distiller, in London in 1684. He died in 1706 and Jane inherited a great deal of wealth from her husband and other members of her family (her brother Thomas Chew died in 1698, her sister Elizabeth Aynscombe died in 1711, another brother William Chew died in 1712, and another sister, Frances Ashton, died in 1727). Jane became a generous benefactress to Dunstable causes and these former almshouses are one of her many gifts to the town.

Like many historic buildings, these almshouses have now been converted into luxury apartments, though only after renovation to meet new safety standards.

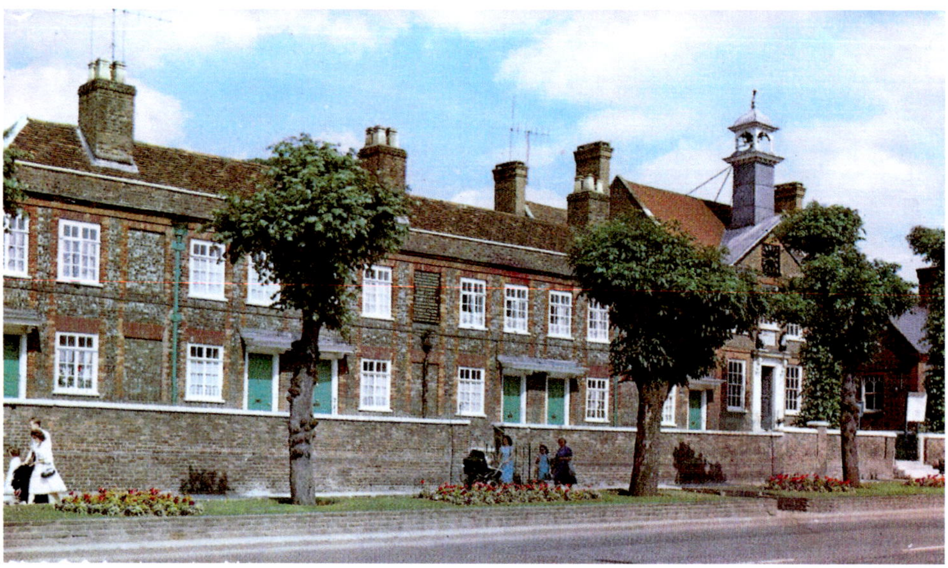

The almshouses with Chew's House next door.

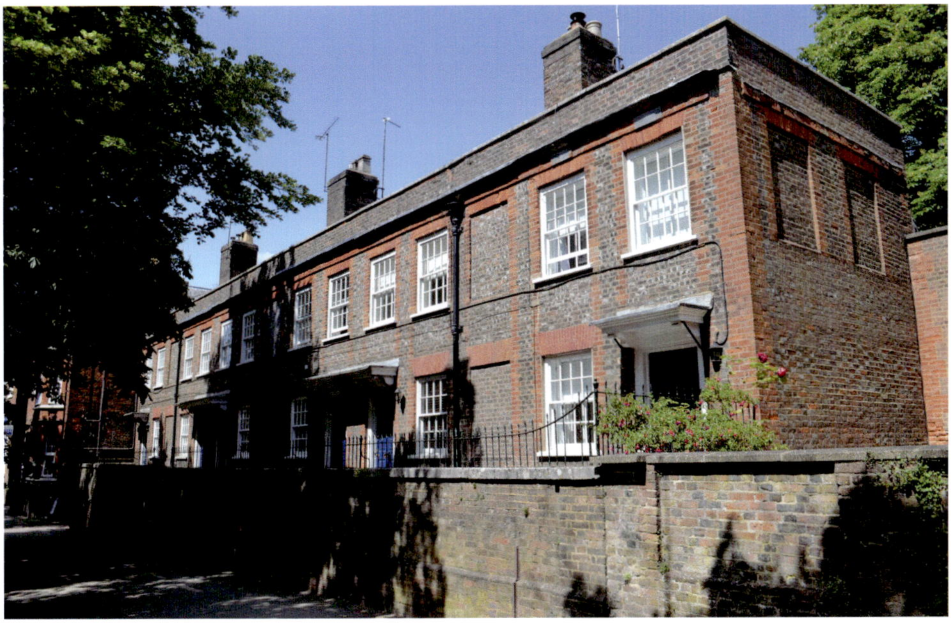

Above: The almshouses today.

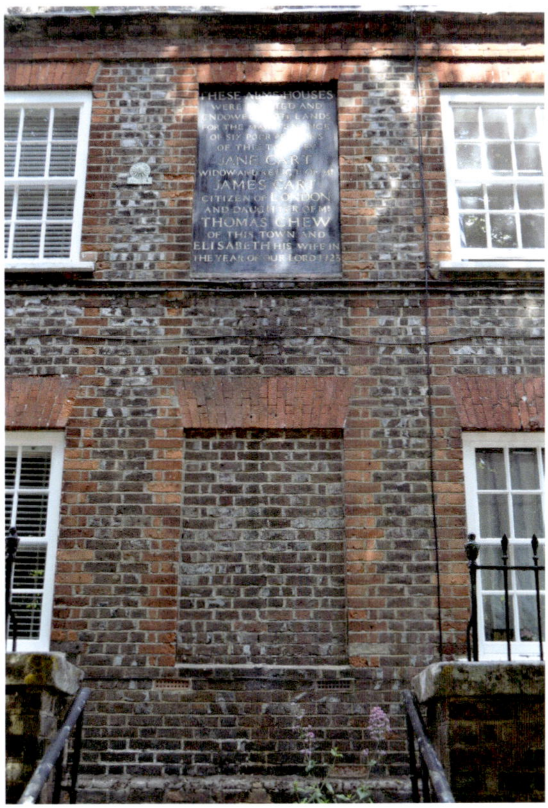

Right: A reminder of past history and origins.

12. Grove House

Another fine building in the town, the current town council offices started life as a public house and coaching inn known as the Duke of Bedford's Arms. This was built by a local builder, John Swindall, and was completed in 1747. The house and estate were acquired by local landowner John Miller and converted into a private residence in the late eighteenth century.

The house was remodelled in the late nineteenth century in the neoclassic style with a heavy stucco finish and involved a symmetrical main frontage with five bays facing onto High Street North. The house, its estate and Park Farm were all acquired by a local businessman Arthur Bagshawe in 1920. Following his death, the house and its enlarged estate were bought by Dunstable Corporation in 1936. The house was converted for use by the corporation as offices and the gardens were opened to the public.

During the Second World War air-raid shelters were established in the gardens. After the war annual garden fêtes were opened by celebrities, including the

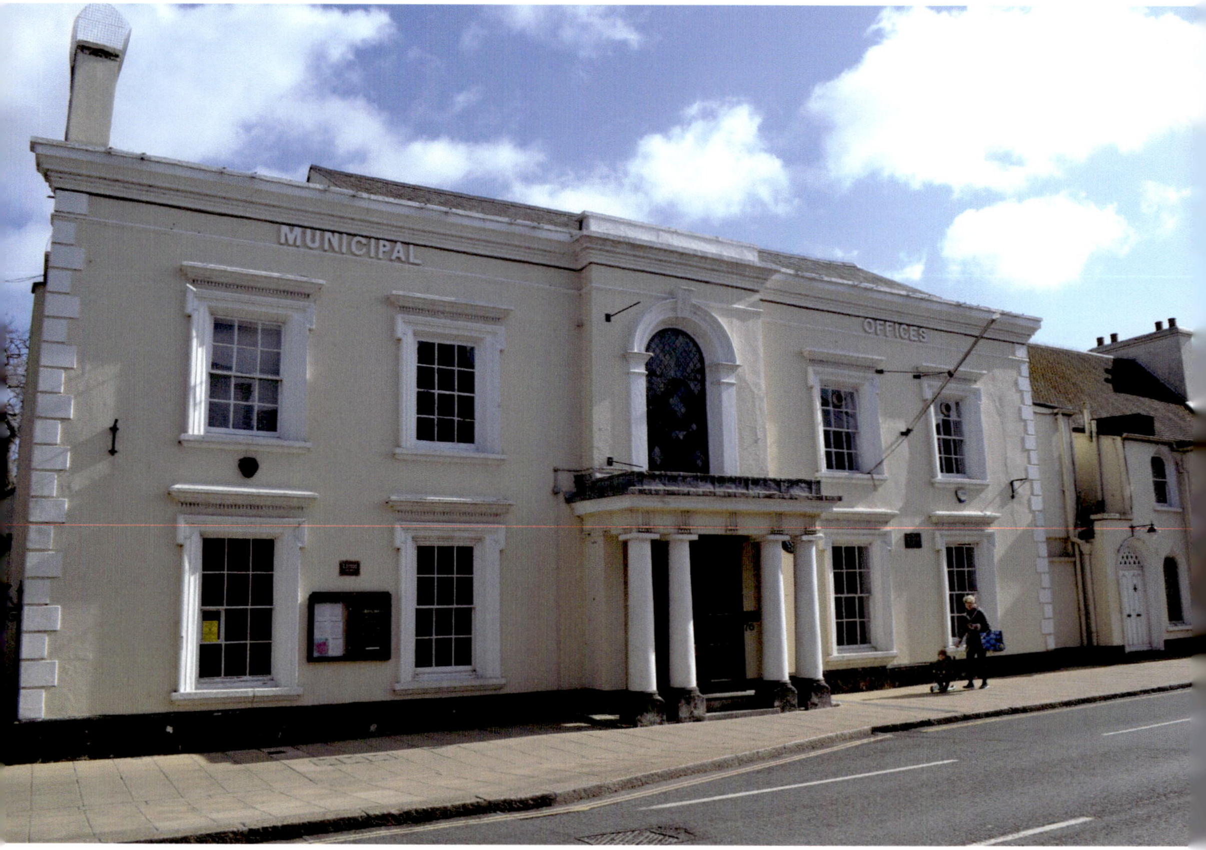

A former coaching inn, the Duke of Bedford's Arms.

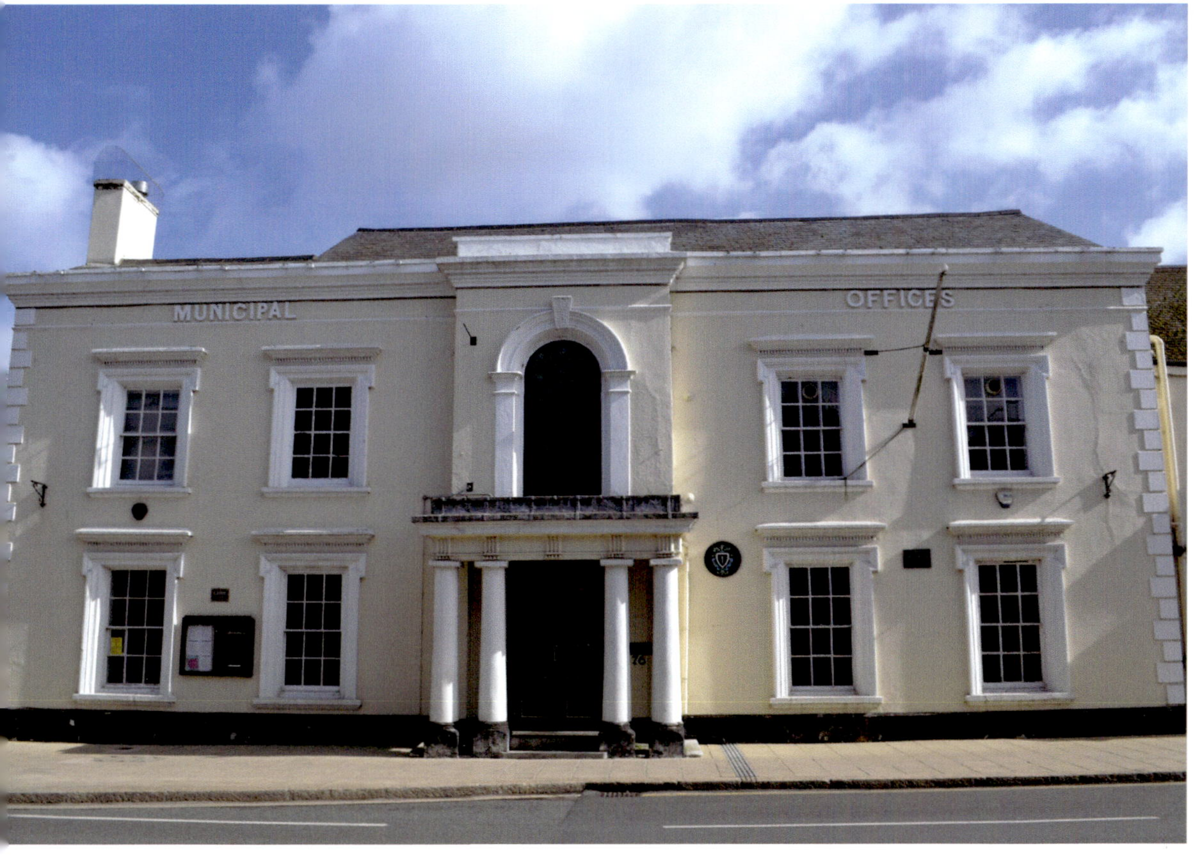

Grove House, the seat of democracy in Dunstable, but once a famous coaching inn.

BBC Radio presenter Derek McCulloch in 1951 and the novelist Barbara Cartland and actor Sam Kydd in 1959.

Following local government reorganisation in 1974, the building was briefly used by South Bedfordshire District Council until it moved to new offices on the site of the former Dunstable North railway station in 1989. The newly formed Dunstable Town Council acquired the building and moved into it at that time. As well as being the offices and meeting place for the town council, it became an approved venue for weddings and civil partnership ceremonies.

13. The Grey House, High Street South

This Georgian town house has had a number of uses over many decades. It was once an inn called the Star, and later a hat factory. The first record of the building as the Star Inn was in 1764 when, according to the Dunstable Parish Register, 'Thomas Groom at ye Star' was buried. A 1773 deed also mentions 'a farm house in Dunstable, formerly called Malting Farm, formerly in the occupation of Benjamin Johnson, now John Shilbourne, and now called the Starr Inn and Farm'. It was not uncommon for inns, alehouses and beerhouses to be attached to small farms to help out with what at times could be a challenging living. During long opening hours, the wife would invariably deal with a few customers whilst the husband would look after poultry and cows or work in the kitchen garden. With so many inns in the town, there was significant competition and therefore not surprising that it did not survive.

By the middle of the nineteenth century part of the house was used as a straw hat and bonnet factory for Luton hat company Munt and Brown. It was leased to Miss Eliza Osborne by 1870, who ran a very successful straw hat business. The top floor would have been a large workroom where women and girls worked. In the basement, the men would have stiffened the hats in baths of gelatine, dried them, then softened them by steam and shaped them on wooden blocks on a blocking machine. In the rear yard of the building was a well or tank containing soft water that was connected to a hand pump in the scullery, which was needed to provide the steam in the basement. The hat factory closed down, along with many others in Dunstable, soon after Luton opened its railway line to London in 1858. By 1910 it was a hotel.

The building changed hands many times at the turn of the century, including being owned and lived in by Thomas Wyatt Bagshaw, Arthur Bagshaw and his

The Grey House, once a hat factory.

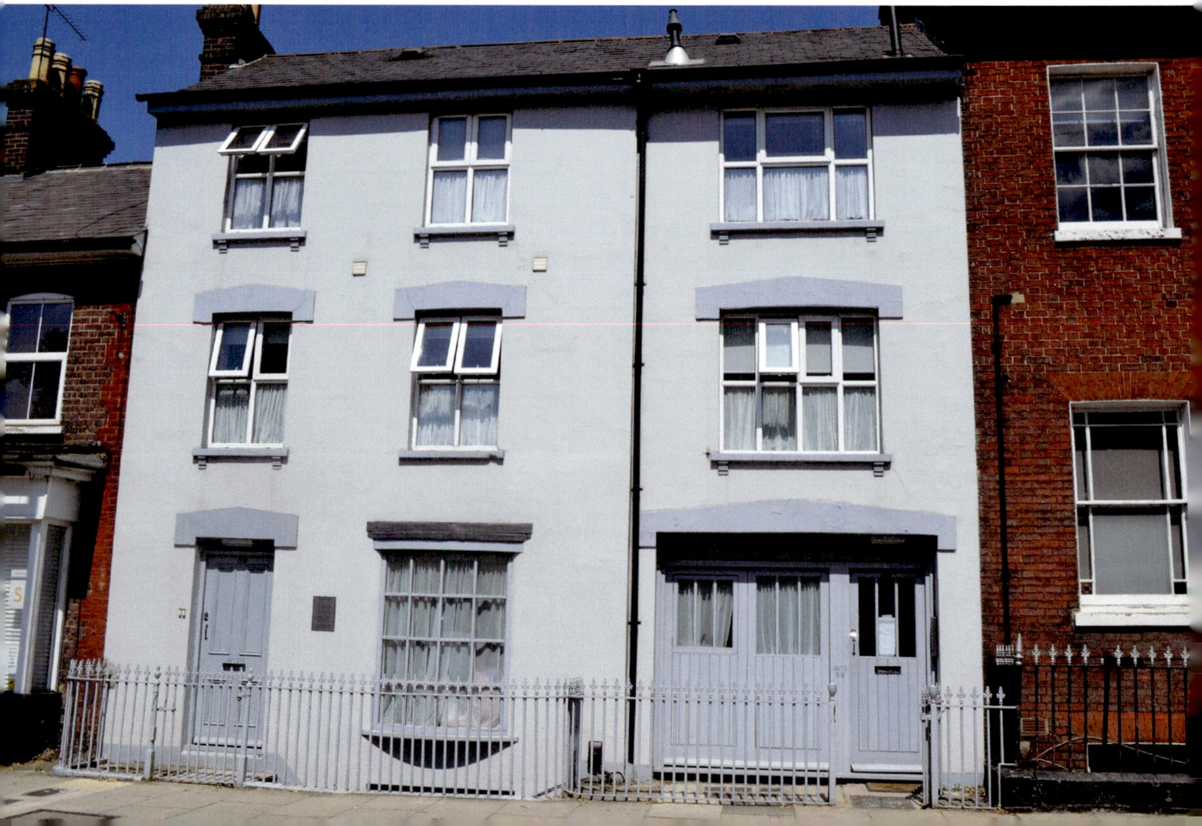

widow Mrs Eliza Bagshaw from 1926 to 1950. The building survived a major catastrophe in 1925 when the Luton Electricity Extension Order was approved for supply to the town and some houses changed from gas to electricity – a short circuit set a gas pipe on fire, but fortunately there was little damage.

In 1952 the premises opened as The Grey House Hotel and was then converted into a private club. By the 1960s it was a reputable fish restaurant, and a bar in the 1980s. In 2016 the building was converted into residential apartments.

14. Marshe Almshouses

Ladies' Lodge is known also as Marshe Almshouses. It is accommodation that was set up from the endowments of Blandina Marshe and Mary Lockington in 1770 for 'poor maiden gentlewomen who should be upwards of 40 years and be descended of reputable parents'.

There are six houses or 'lodges', each of which is designed for single long-term habitation. Space was also provided for visitors to stay overnight. Each lodge has its own back yard for hanging washing and housing rubbish bins. There is a large communal rear garden for residents' use. A gardener tends the front and rear gardens. The building was constructed circa 1743 with a stucco frontage and includes a tympanum which contains a circular panel with a coat of arms

Marshe Almshouses.

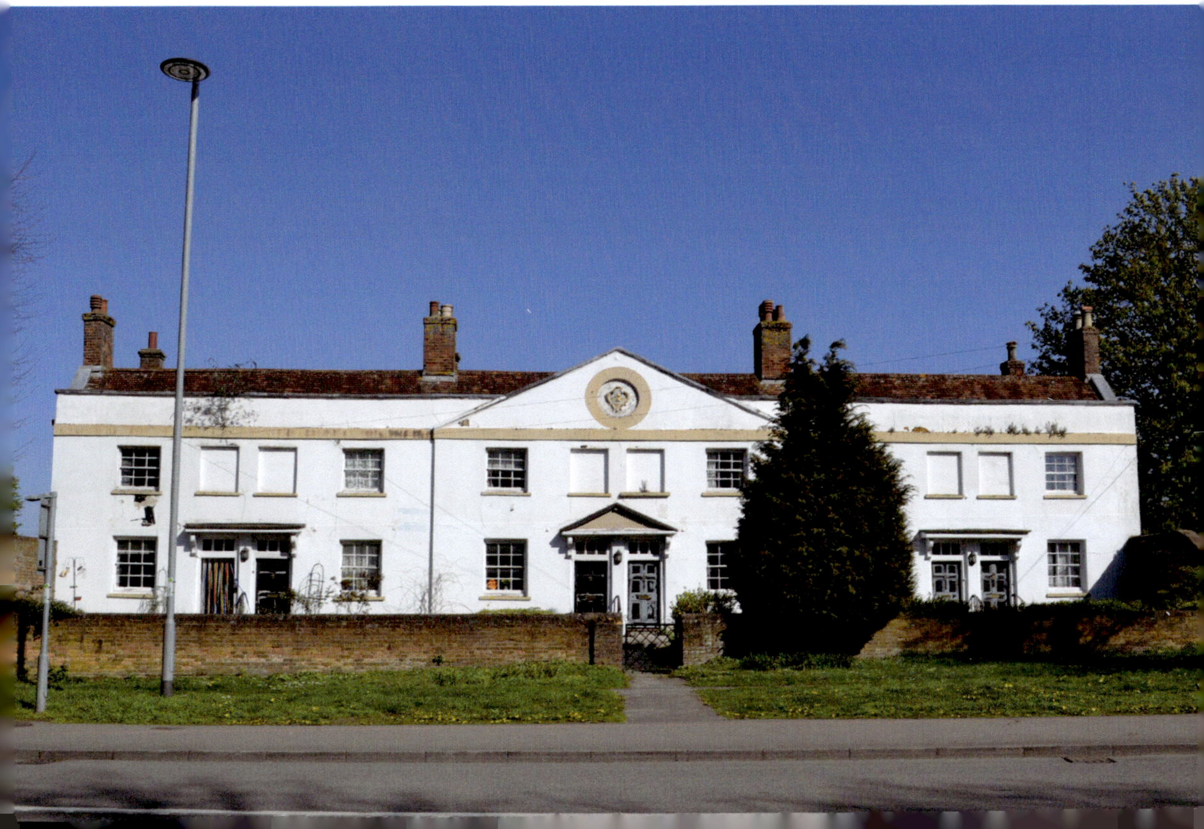

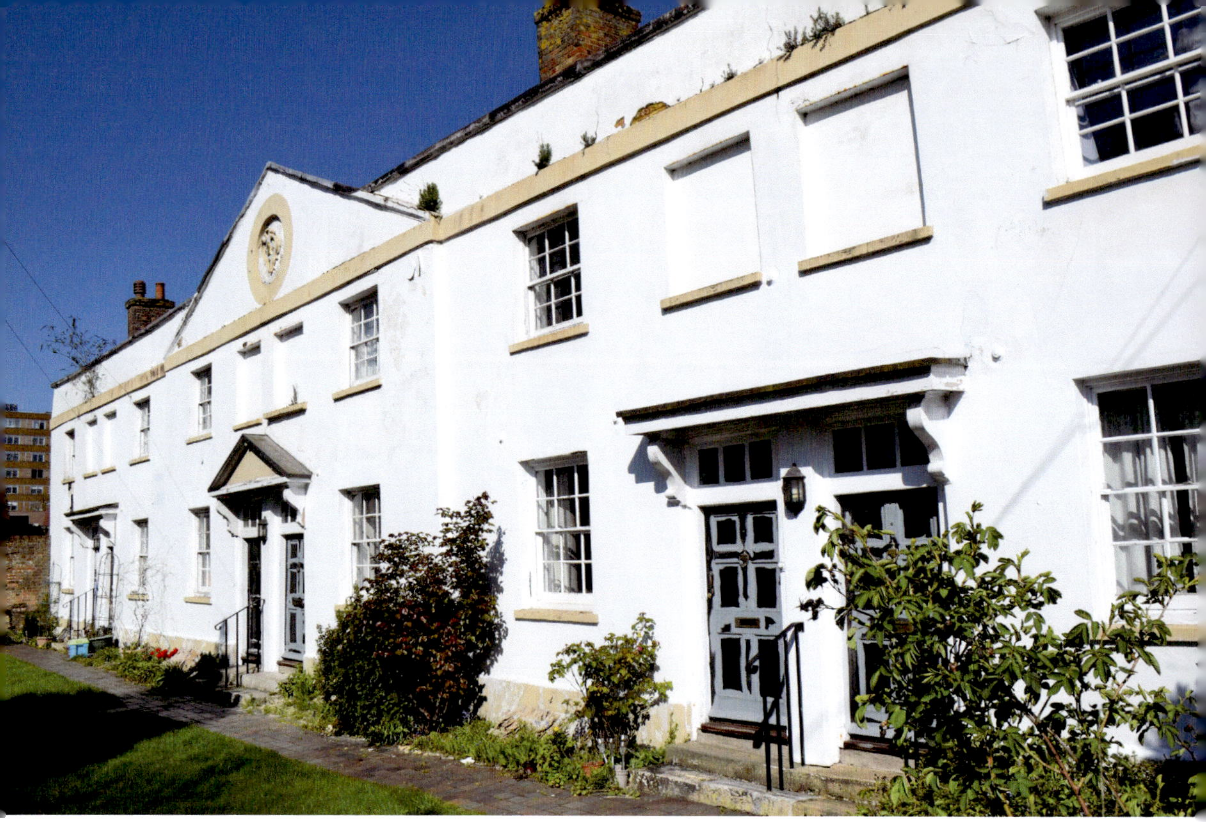

Above: Marshe Almshouses set up for 'poor maiden gentlewomen'.

Below: The coat of arms and inscription.

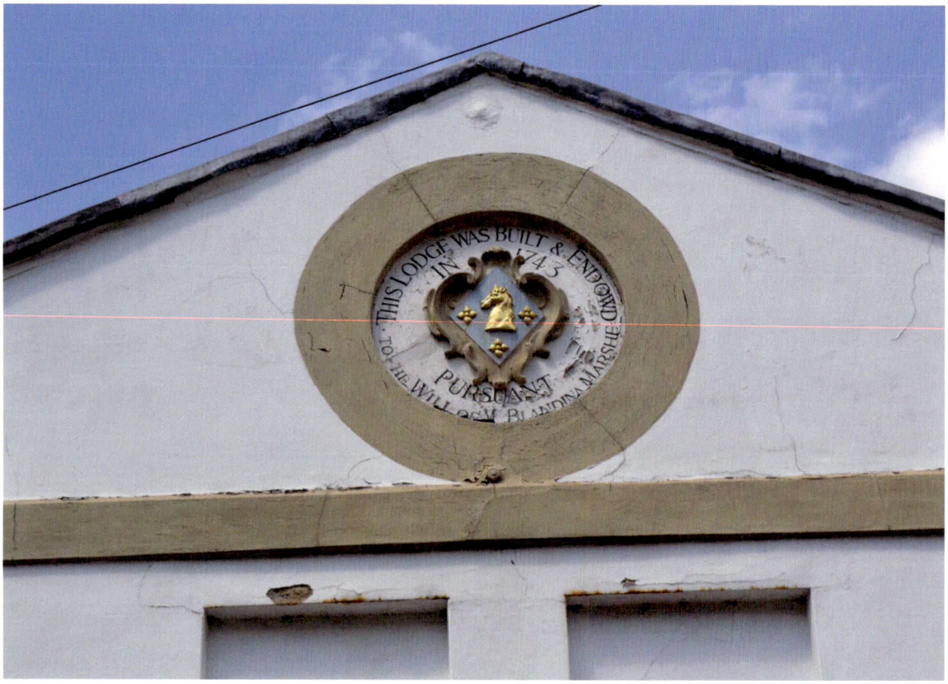

and inscription: 'This Lodge was built and endowed pursuant to the Will of Mrs Blandina Marshe'.

Blandina Marshe (1663–1741) was the unmarried daughter of John Marshe (1617–1700) and Blandina (née Iremonger). Mary Lockington (1663–1730) was the sister of Blandina Marshe and the wife of Thomas Lockington. Blandina and Mary made provisions in their wills for charities to be set up to help the poor. Along with the support for the 'six maiden gentlewomen', she also left an annual sum of £5 to be paid from her Kingsbury Farm estate to poor people who attended church. The charity continued through money gained from land and property that had been left for this purpose, including a farm at Toddington and two cottages.

Mary Lockington's charity included money for poor maids, poor clergymen's widows. The money was also gained from land, including 102 acres at Totternhoe, 95 acres at Toddington, 59 acres at Hockliffe and Eggington, 3 acres at Stanbridge and 61 acres at Soulbury in Buckinghamshire.

15. No. 20 High Street North, now the Nationwide Building Society

At first glance the building at No. 20 High Street North would barely warrant further attention. Now home to a branch of Nationwide building society, it was once a well-known retail outlet called Charlie Cole's Bicycle Shop from 1925 to 1985, until he moved to High Street South. Charlie's penny-farthing used to protrude at right angles to these old premises and was a popular landmark in the centre of the town. The shop was almost fully rebuilt in 1985, but it was based on a very old timber-framed building that dated from the sixteenth century. It was at one time part of an inn, possibly The Bear.

It is a listed building due to a collection of wall paintings on six panels of the first-floor party wall, which depict a hunting scene with other motives in an overall verdure tapestry background. These were discovered in 1954 during alterations. The panels contain a small rabbit, a man dressed in Tudor clothing smoking a long clay pipe or blowing a hunting horn, a cock's head, a running stag, a greyhound and the figure of a man. They date from around 1580, with some of these now displayed on the ground floor.

Charlie Cole was very well known locally. He was born in 1900 and dedicated his life to racing and selling bicycles. In June 1970, at the age of seventy, he won two classic races for veteran cyclists: a 30-mile race at the National Championships and a 25-mile trial on the Isle of Man. In 1985, he celebrated sixty years in business, and he was still cycling at the age of eighty-five years old.

Before this, however, until 1785 the building was the White Hart Inn, which had been recorded on the site in 1606. Later it became the home of Thomas Collings's family, who purchased it in about 1821. He later also bought the adjoining property. Collings was a watch and clock maker as well as a straw hat manufacturer. His factory stood at the back. The property went on the market

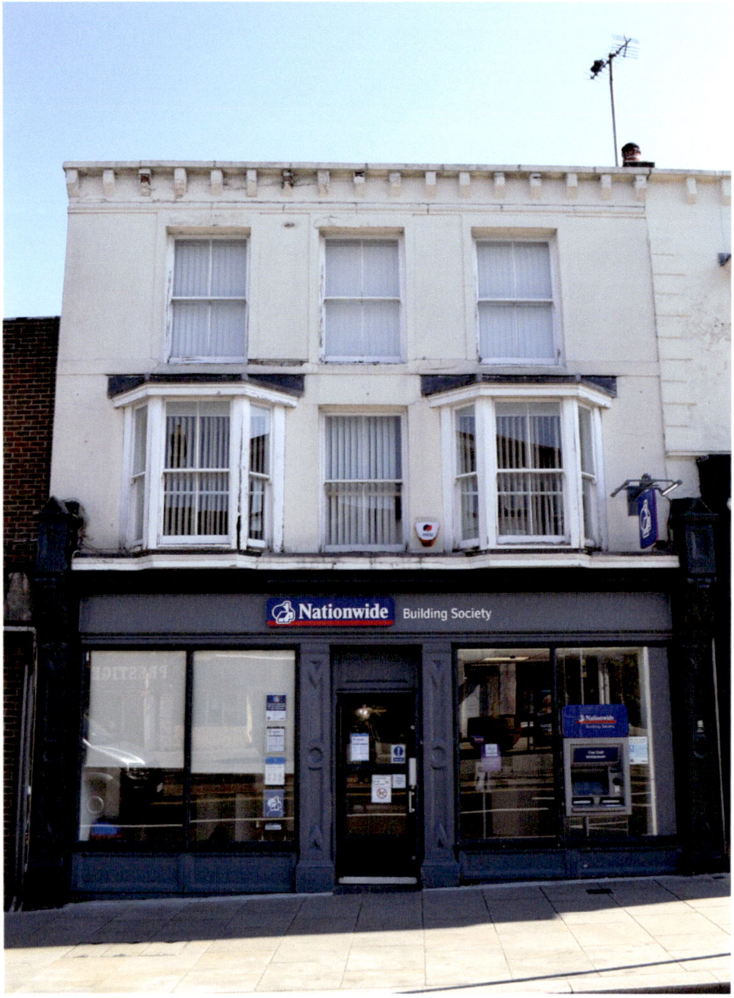

Once Charlie Cole's bicycle shop, the building at No. 20 High Street North has a long history in the town.

after Thomas's death. The house (No. 18) was known as Collingswood House and was sold in 1914. This was also the site of Rose Harlow's popular Confectionary Bazaar. No. 20 later became the Misses Wilson's hat shop (before they moved), and in 1933 it then became the locally famous Charlie Cole's cycle shop. In the 1980s it was taken over by Nationwide, which remains to this day.

16. The Friars, High Street South

The Friars is located on the corner of Friars Walk and High Street South, at the southern end of the Square. It was named after the friary that was in this area between the thirteenth and sixteenth centuries. The actual site of the main friary buildings is now covered by the nearby industrial estate and the houses

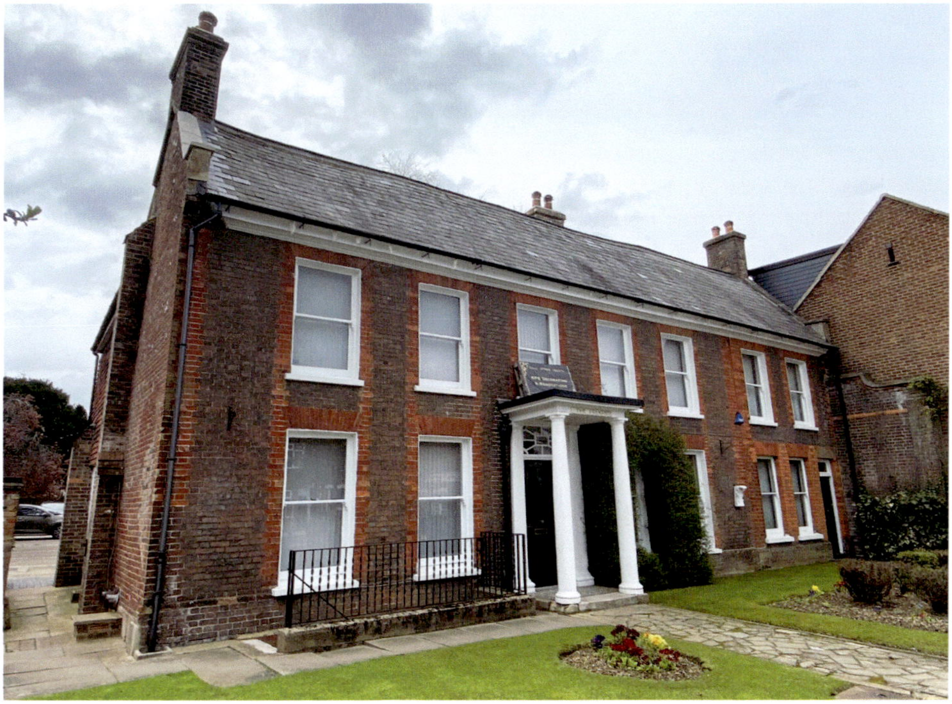

The Friars on High Street South.

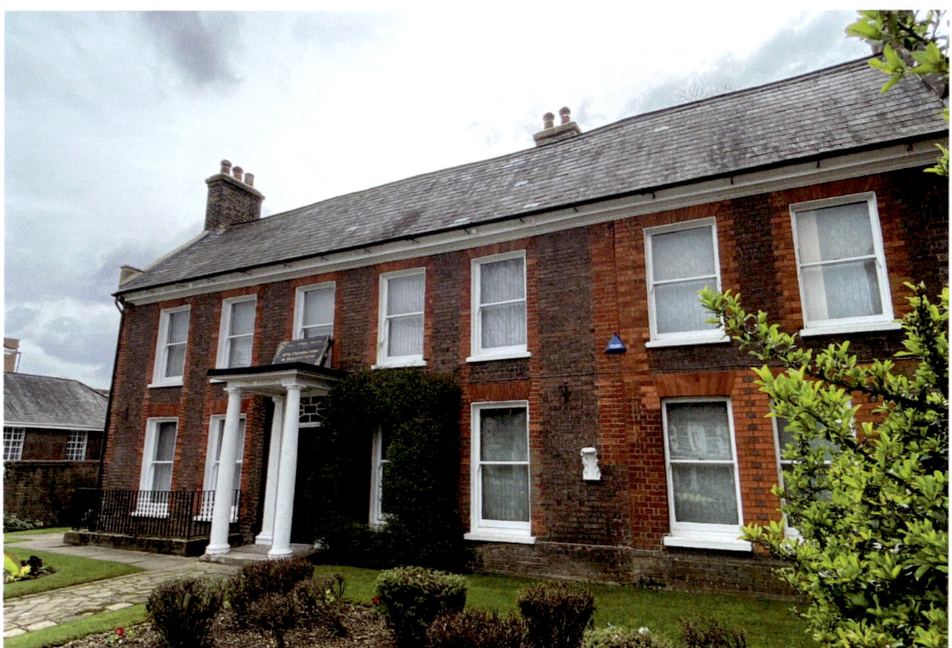

The Friars undergoing renovation in 2023.

off Bullpond Lane. Originally a private residence for local wealthy people, from 1985 it was the home of Dunstable Town Council. Prior to that it was owned and occupied by a company called Air Call who were based in Houghton Regis.

Little is known about the early life of this building. It is probably early nineteenth century and possibly built on the site of an older house. It was also known as Queensborough House after a local family of that name.

17. Priory Church Hall

This pretty little building was originally built in 1839 as the National School for Infants, which closed in 1922 and was formally reopened in 1926 as the Church Hall.

In 1833 the government decided to award annual grants towards education, but unfortunately there was very little support for any kind of national education policy, so grants awarded were very small. In 1833 there was only £20,000 allocated for the whole country.

With the lack of government action, two groups were established to organise schools and use the little amount of money that was available. These were the Anglican National Society (for national schools) and the Nonconformist British and Foreign Society (for British schools). Dunstable had both Anglicans and

Priory Church Hall, once an important local school.

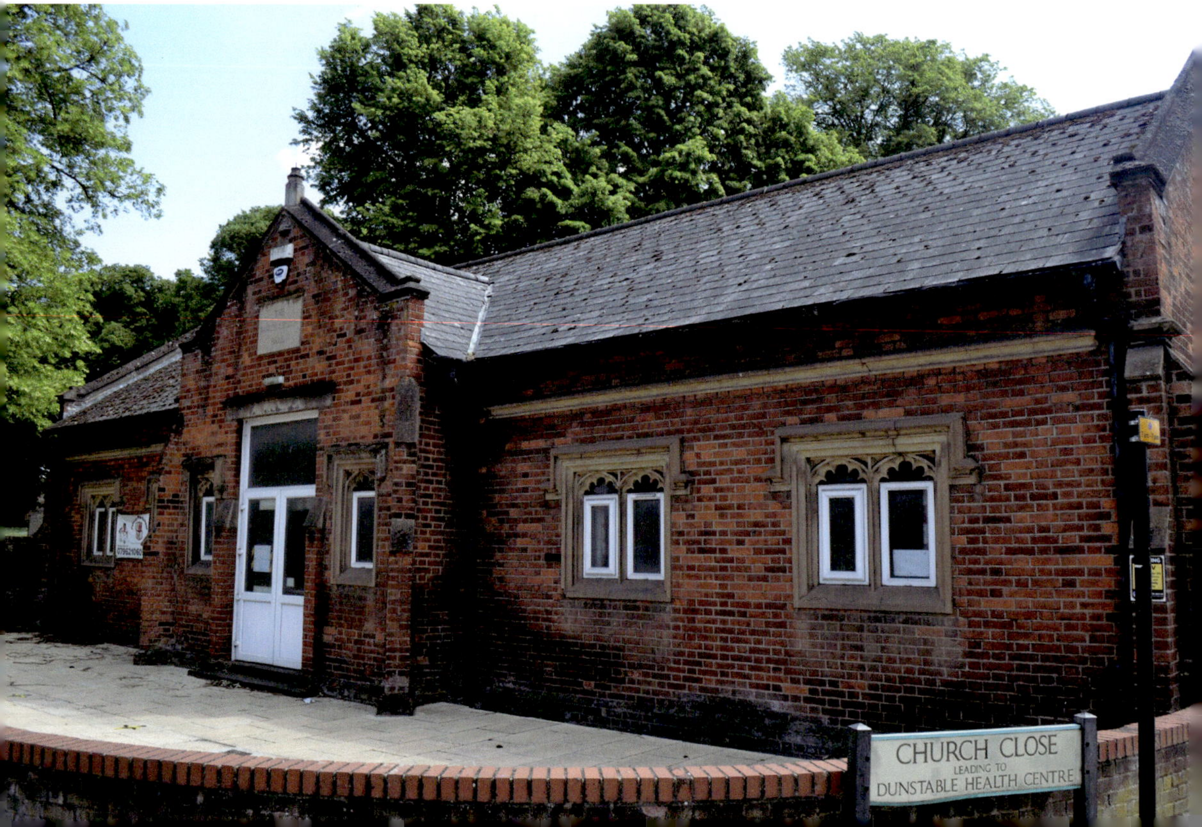

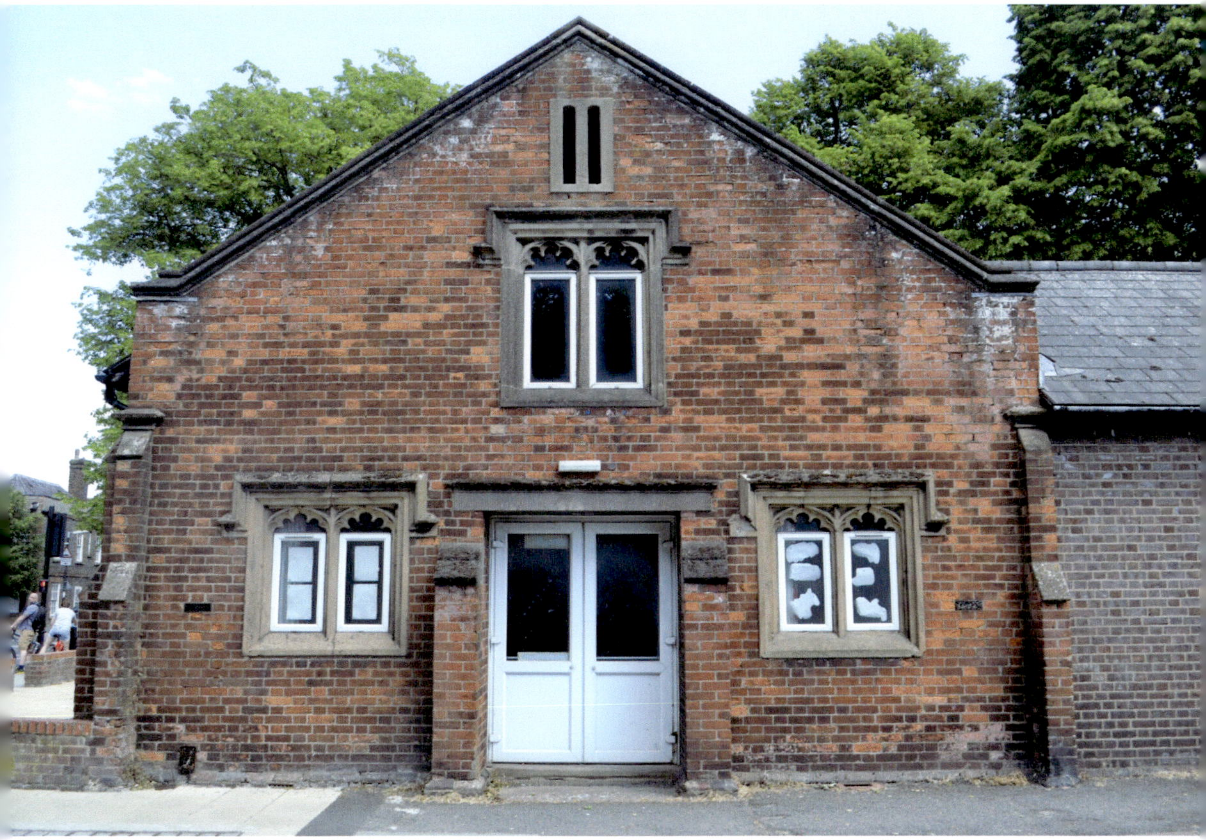

Priory Church Hall, still used today as a community facility.

Nonconformists, so both national and British schools were established. As a result, the National School was founded in Church Street and the British School was founded in West Street at the Baptist Church.

The National School opened here in 1839 for 250 pupils and was aimed at providing an education for the poor. Initially, the infants received no more education after leaving this school. From 1864, however, infants from the National School were able to go on to the Ashton Junior School which was opposite. Attendance was voluntary until the 1870 Education Act was passed, after which all infants should have been at school. Unfortunately, many children did not attend as they were often engaged in the hat plaiting industry. By 1894, the National School was advertised as being designed for 140 pupils with 'an average attendance of 101'. The school eventually was closed in 1922 with infants attending schools in Burr Street and Chiltern Road.

From 1926, the school building became the parish hall of the Priory Church and has been used for Sunday schools, Scout and Guide groups, Mother's Union, youth clubs and other community functions since then.

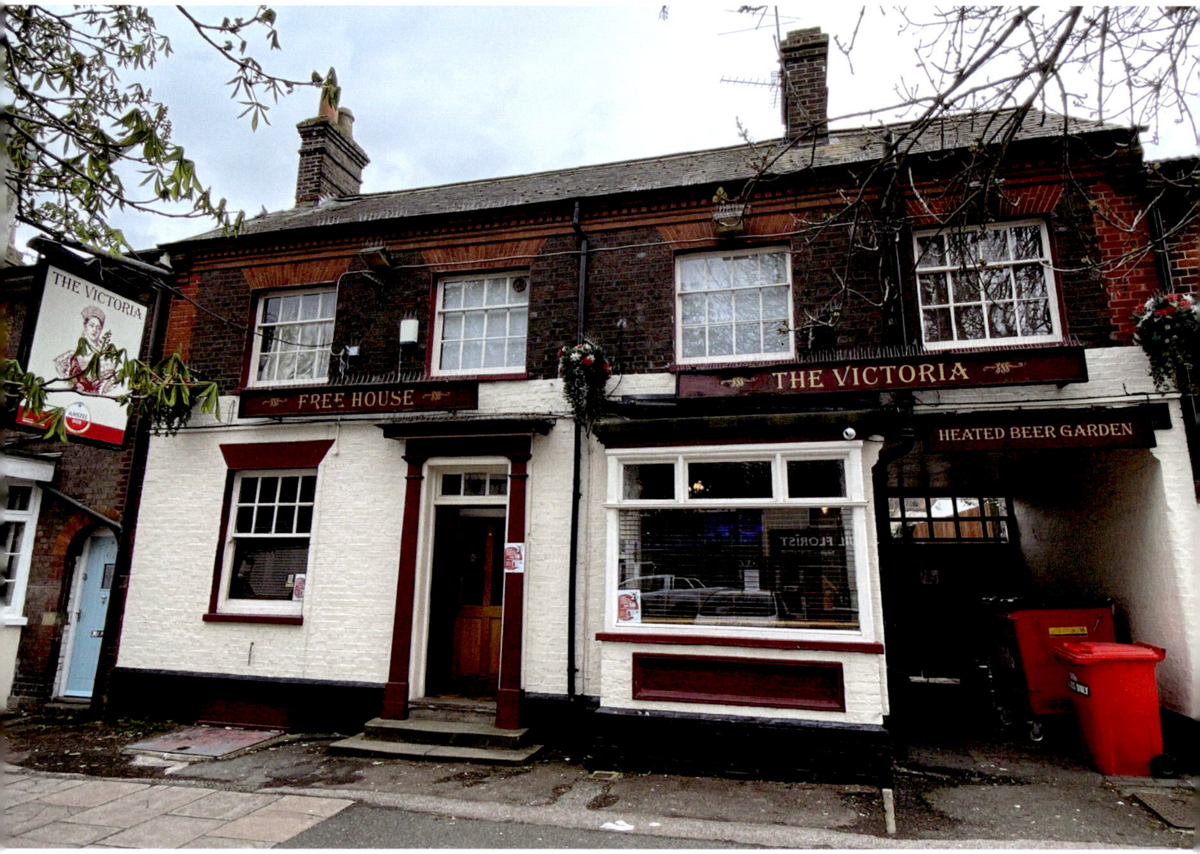

The Victoria public house.

18. The Victoria Public House, West Street

The tree-lined road of West Street currently hides a pleasant Victorian public house called, surprisingly, The Victoria. It was built during the reign of Queen Victoria and sits opposite Victoria Street. Queen Victoria visited Dunstable with her husband Prince Albert in 1841 when she visited an exhibition of local lace and straw plait work at the nearby Sugar Loaf Hotel. The queen was of particular importance to the town as it was she who sold the townsfolk the town hall in 1866, then the whole manor of Dunstable in 1870.

19. The Former Borough Arms, Albion Street

Over the centuries Dunstable has had many public houses and inns. While a number have survived, such as the Sugar Loaf, many have closed as times and recreational activities have changed. Sadly, the majority of them have either been

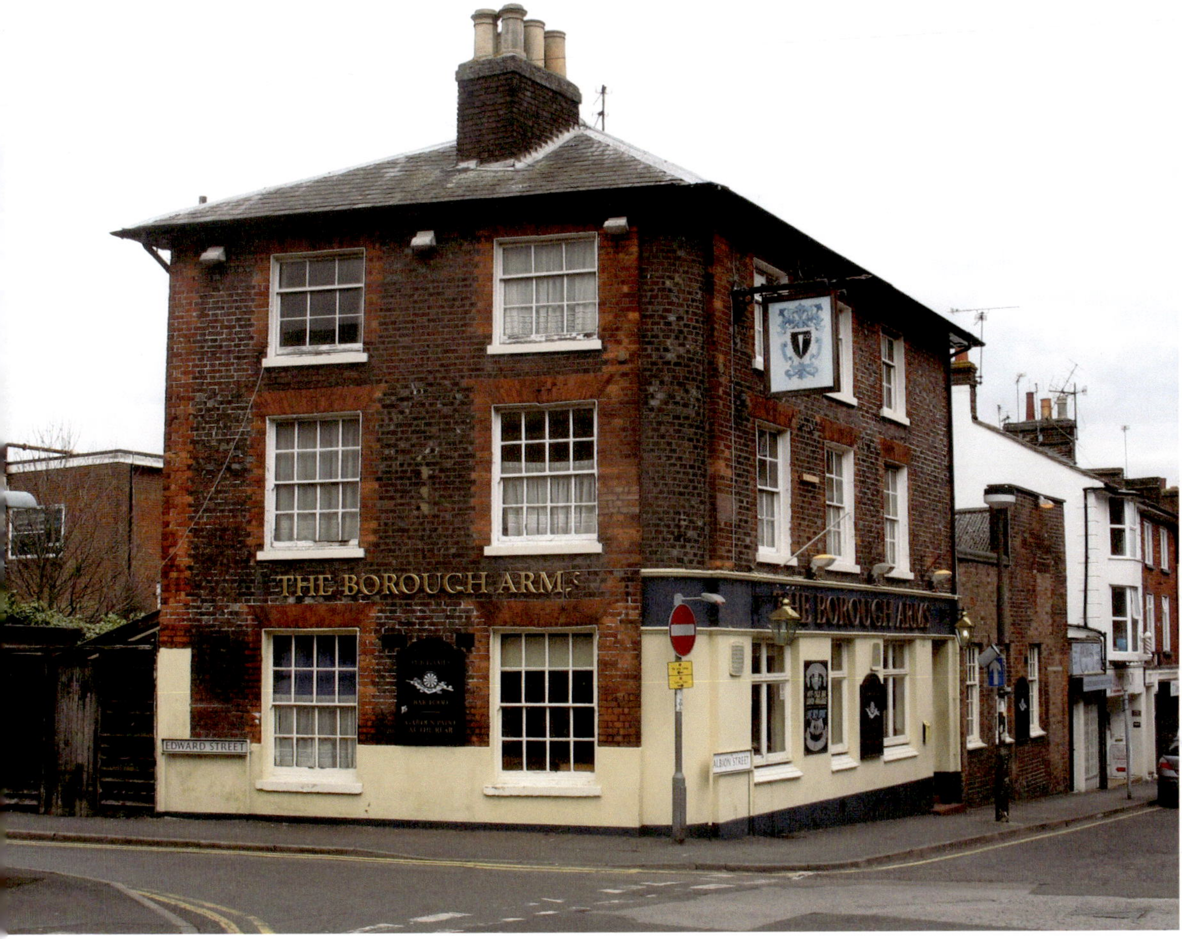

The Borough Arms, taken in 2008 by Kevin Lane, just before it closed the following year.

demolished or changed beyond all recognition, whilst others await a new future. The global pandemic of 2020 also significantly affected the viability of many public houses too, not just locally but across the country.

One of the finest buildings on the back streets of Dunstable, however, was saved from demolition. The former Borough Arms on Albion Street is a Grade II listed building and dates from the early to mid-nineteenth century. In 1850, the site of the pub was sold by Edward Burr to Frederick Burr, who built a small coaching inn called the Crown with adjoining stables. By 1853, the Crown was advertised as an inn and posting house and occupied by Henry Lockhart, beer retailer and coach proprietor. However, by 1862 Henry Lockhart had moved to the nearby Red Lion Hotel.

It was still certainly a public house in the 1871 census but had been renamed the Borough Arms. It had a succession of landlords over many years, including Edwin Tilley, who was there from at least 1914 until the early 1930s. It was

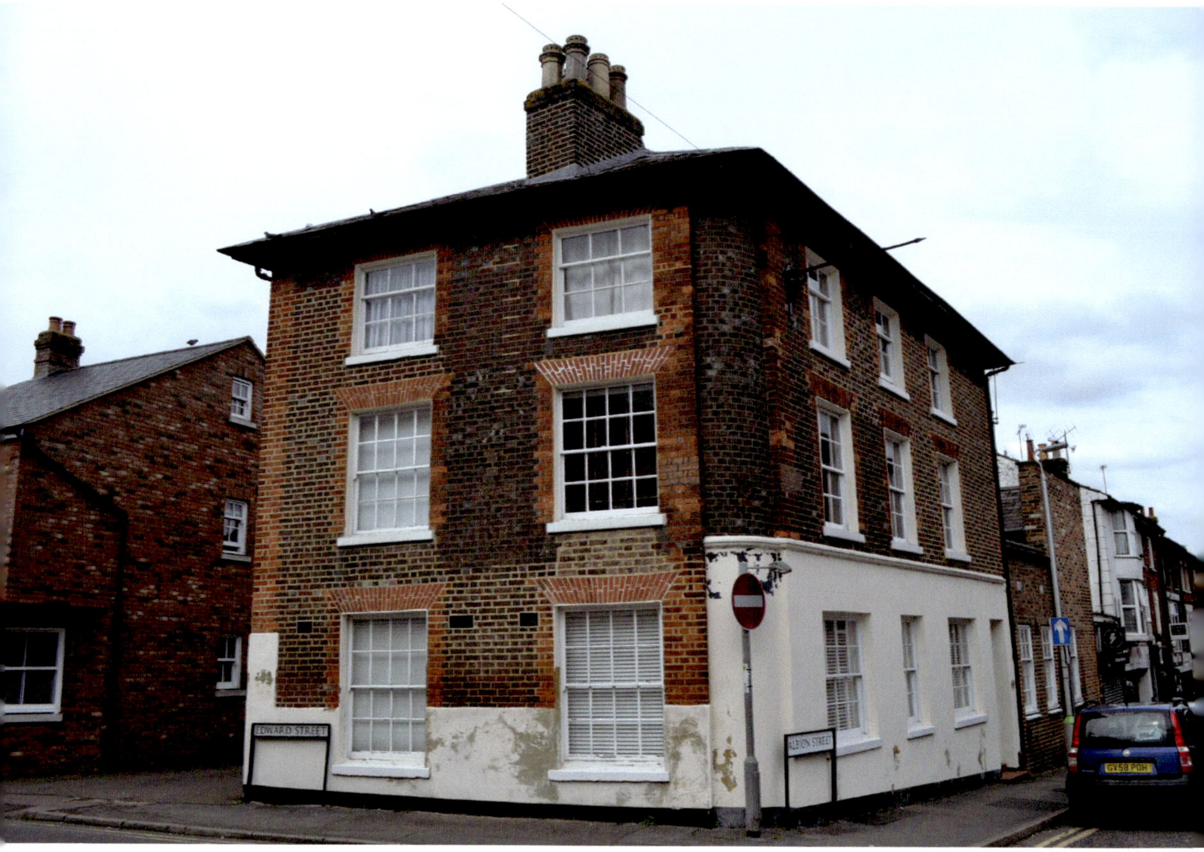

The Borough Arms, now residential on Albion Street.

modernised in the mid-1980s and was extended into the old stables next door. The Borough Arms eventually closed in 2009 after being known as Goffys Bar for a while. It has since been restored for residential use in this popular street, its history long since gone.

20. West Street Mill

The old windmill in West Street was built in 1839 for local landowner Richard Gutteridge. The sails were removed in 1908 after the mill owner discovered that it was more reliable to grind corn using steam power. An engine had been added so that milling could continue when there was insufficient wind to turn the sails. The mill continued to grind corn for miller Frank Simmons until just before the Second World War, when it was used as an observation post by the Home Guard.

The mill became the headquarters of the Dunstable Sea Cadets in 1948. Admiral Sir Lionel Preston, who moved to live in Dunstable (in High Street North) in 1935,

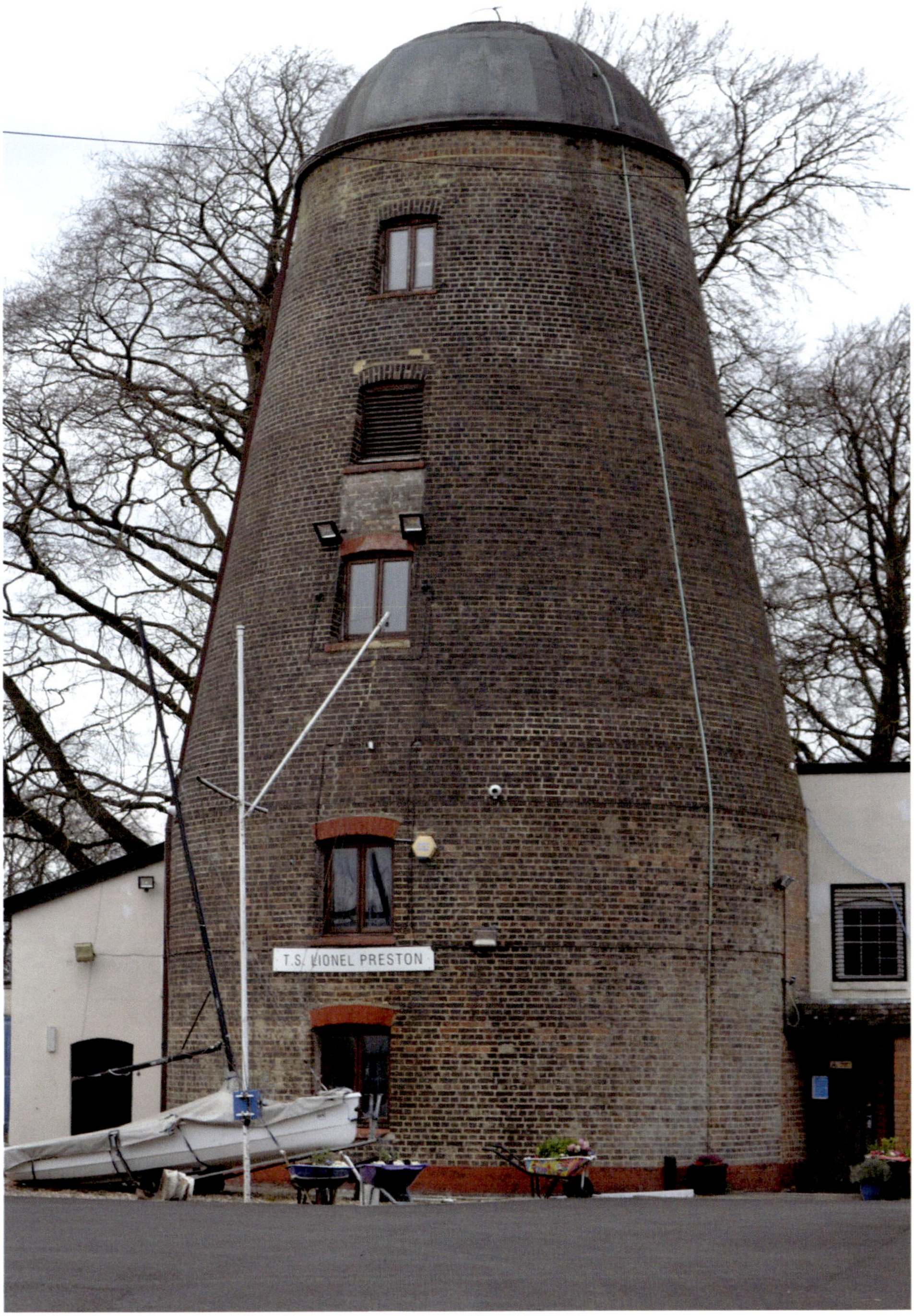

The old West Street Mill.

was instrumental in forming a sea cadet unit as part of the Pioneer Boys Club in 1942, and when the cadets eventually gained their own building it was named Training Ship Lionel Preston in his honour. Sir Lionel died in 1971.

21. Former Carpenter's Arms, High Street South

The Carpenter's Arms in High Street South, with a distinctive coat of arms still visible above its front door, was recorded as being a public house in the nineteenth century and into the 1920s. By the Second World War it had ceased to be a public house and was a private residence.

Its history as a public house does raise a few questions though. It was unlikely to have been a pub in the usual sense, but was most likely an example of a house owned by a tradesman who sometimes sold beer in addition to his own work. The owner, in this instance, was probably a carpenter who also brewed beer. The Carpenter's Arms shield is therefore likely to have been a later addition and would have been a convenient sign that simply referred to a carpenter who sold

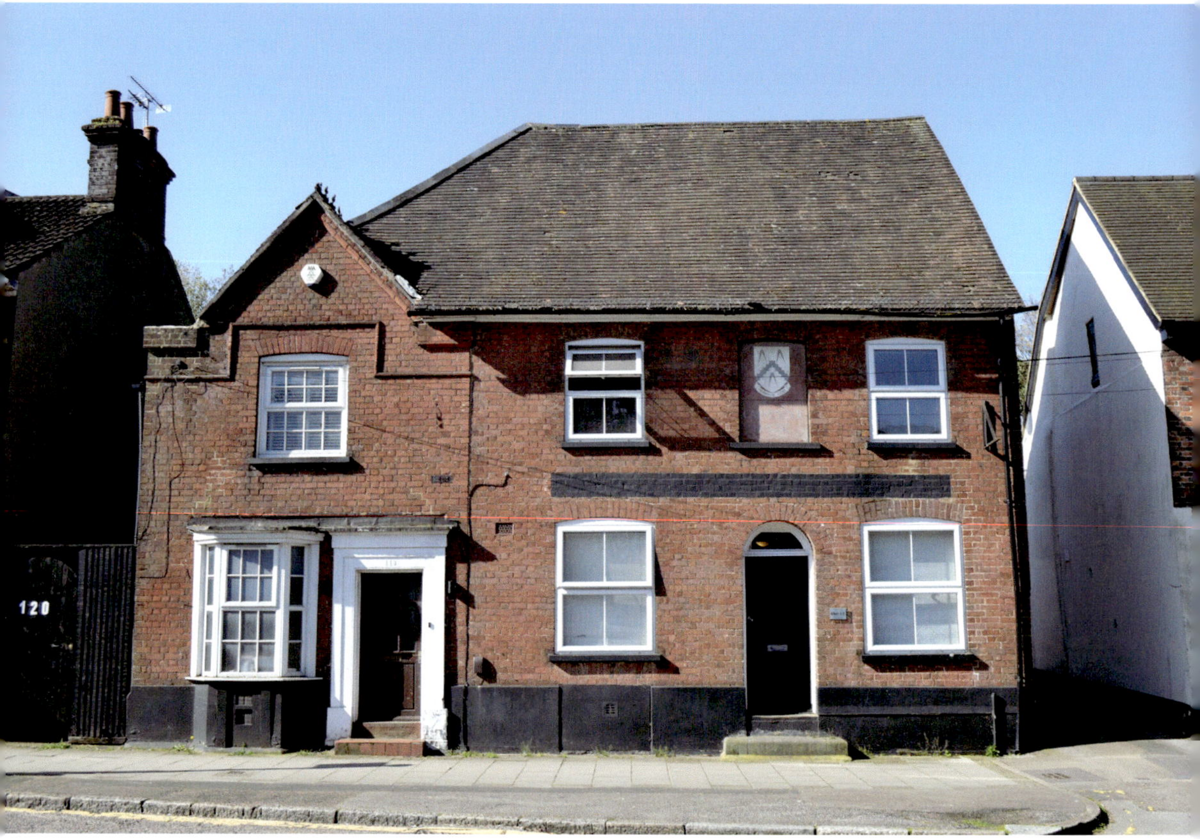

The former Carpenter's Arms.

beer, rather than being a bona fide member of a trades institution. This was not uncommon; similar examples include the Blacksmiths Arms, which earlier in the twentieth century was in West Street and owned by a blacksmith and whitesmith, named Costin, who was also a brewer. People would simply sit in the hallway of his house, with the door closed, and quietly sip their pints of beer. It is now a dentist surgery, but still retains its original name.

22. Congregational Chapel, Edward Street

The Congregational Chapel in Edward Street was opened for worship in January 1854. Congregationalists in the area bought the land in 1852 and erected a temporary wooden building known as The Tabernacle, the first minister there

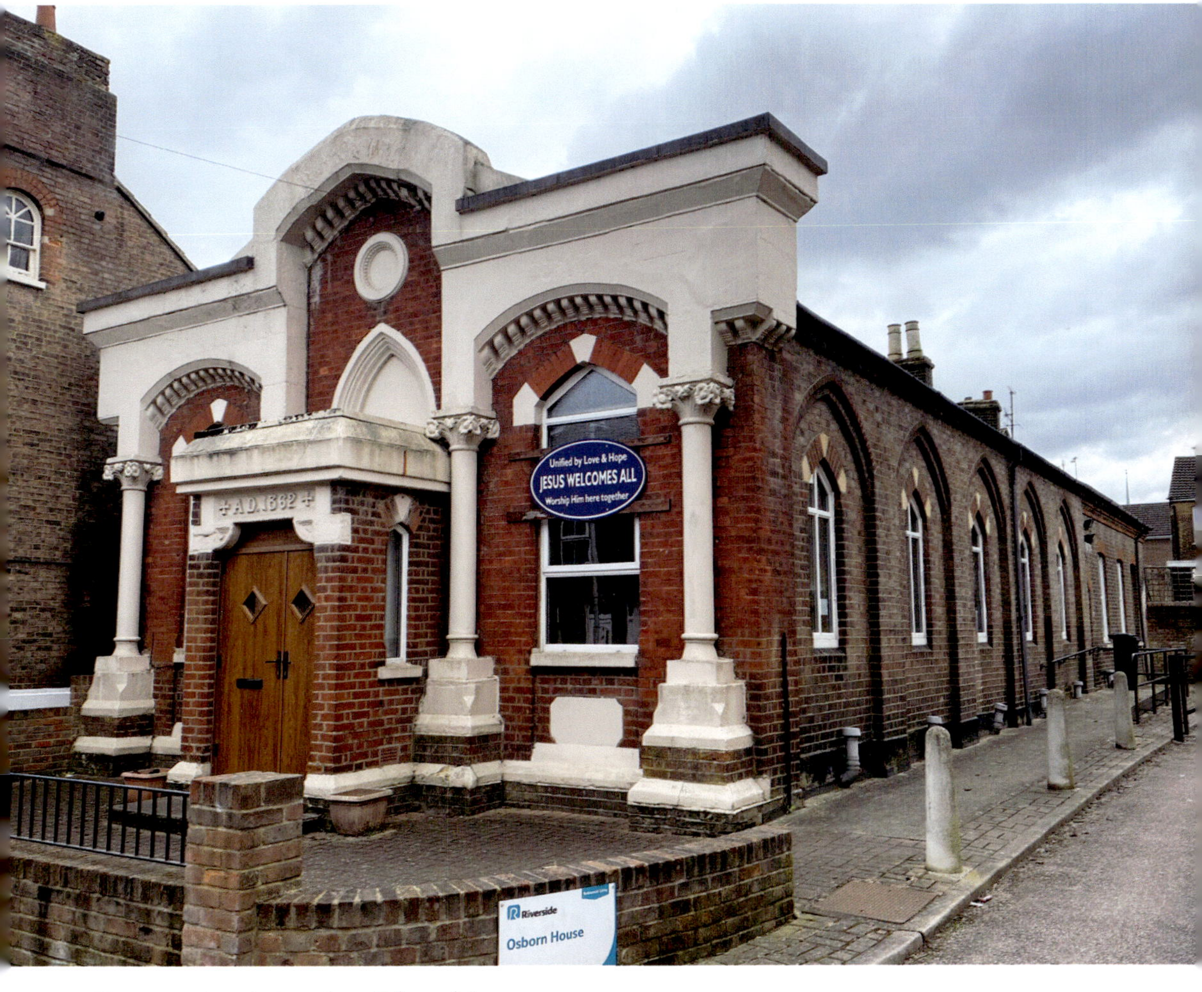

Congregational chapel on Edward Street.

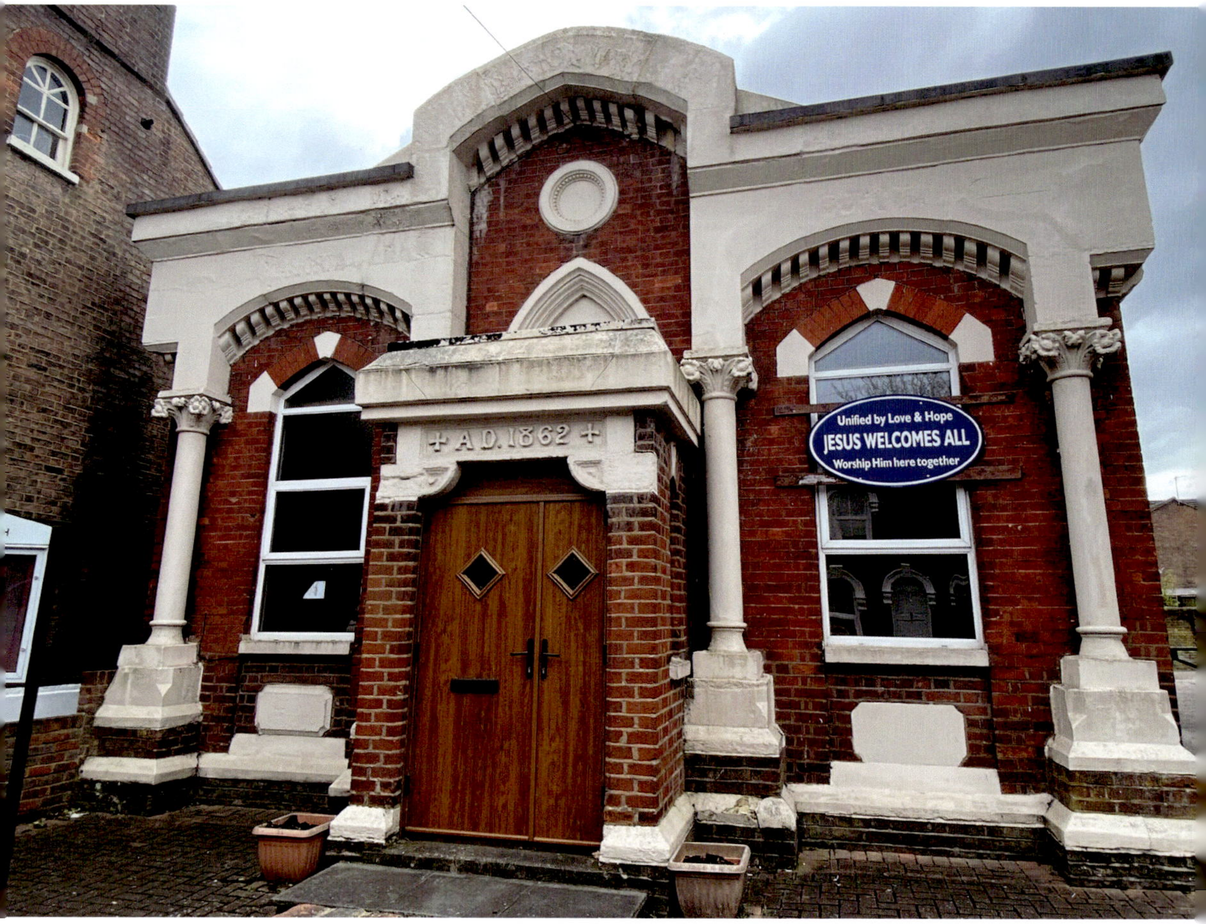

The chapel looks wholly out of place among the adjacent terraced houses.

being Revd Henry Perfect. The foundation stone of the more permanent building was laid in 1853. It later became the United Reformed Church.

The United Reformed Church in Edward Street was originally a school hall attached to the Congregational Church next door. The hall, first known as Osborn Hall in memory of Joseph Osborn, a founder member, was built in 1856. The words on front of the building are 'Bicentenary Memorial School AD 1862'. At the time of writing the building was up for sale.

23. The Former Dunstable Borough Gazette Office

The building on the corner of Albion Street and High Street North was once the offices of the *Dunstable Borough Gazette*. The newspaper's editorial office was on the first floor, and the living accommodation on the top floor at one stage housed

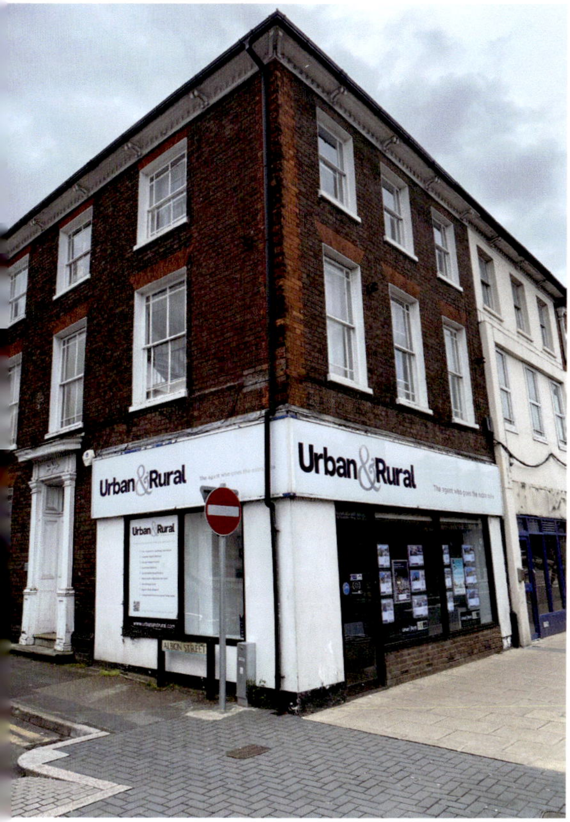

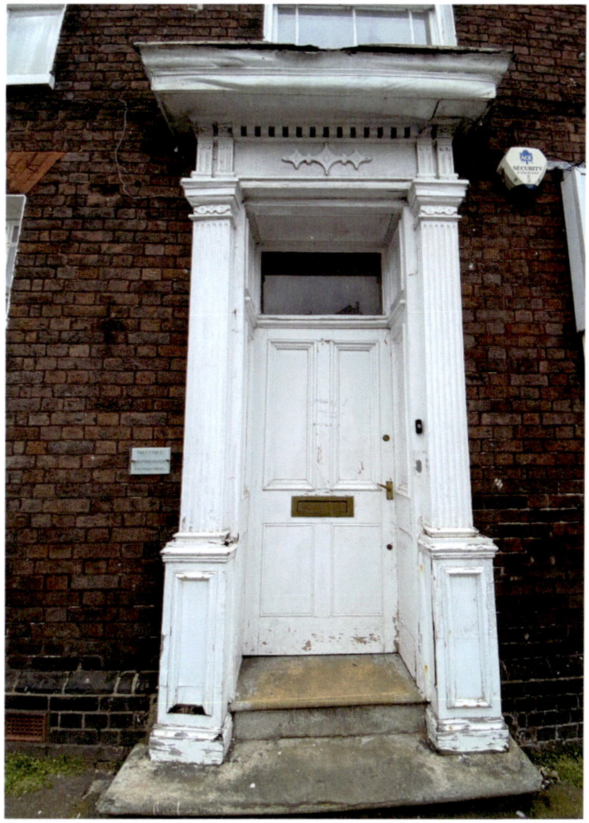

Above left: The former offices of the *Dunstable Borough Gazette*.

Above right: The Printing Works were at the rear of the building.

the town's first telephone exchange. There was a printing works at the rear of the building, but by the mid-1930s the paper was being produced at the *Luton News* printing works in Alma Street, Luton. The *Gazette* had been at No. 39 High Street North since 1879, having moved there from its original premises on the other side of the High Street, near what is now the entrance to the Quadrant. The building is now used by the Urban and Rural estate agents. Next door were the old Liberal Club premises, which became a bookmaker's shop.

24. The Former Dunstable Grammar School

Almost out of character for the High Street North is the old Dunstable Grammar School, which was established by the trustees of the Almshouse Charity created by the will of Frances Ashton, hence the inscription on the building that says: 'Dunstable Grammar School Founded A.D. 1728 By

Mrs. Frances Ashton Built A.D. 1887'. The school was established using money provided by the estate of Mrs Frances Ashton, who died in 1727. She had made numerous bequests to Dunstable, which included provision for the Ashton Almshouses and the primary school in Church Street, but there was a considerable windfall when some of the Ashton land was purchased to build the railway between Dunstable and Luton, and this extra money enabled the grammar school to be built.

The school buildings were constructed in 1887 on the northern side of Dunstable for the trustees of Frances Ashton's charity, and in 1888 the school opened with forty-nine pupils. The first headmaster was L. C. R. Thring, who was of the Thring family of Uppingham which also included the educationist Edward Thring (1821–87), headmaster of Uppingham School. By 1917, the school had grown to sixty-seven boarders and 100 daytime boys. A school library was built in memory of the former pupils who died in the Boer War and the Second World War, and a memorial in the library commemorated the names of the sixty-two boys who gave their lives, including Ashton Edward Thring, the only son of the school's first headmaster, and the Victoria Cross winner Lieutenant Colonel Edward Henderson.

Located behind the school was Park Farm, commonly known as Dunstable Park. Between High Street North and West Street was a large open tract of ground

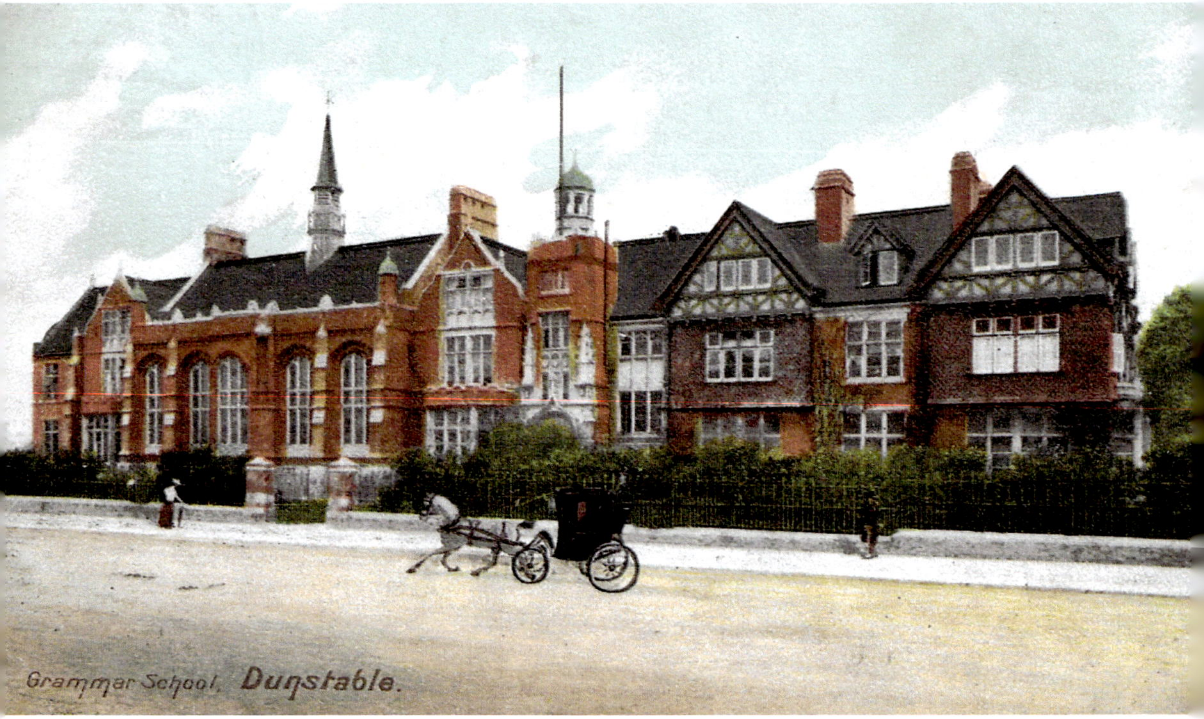

The former Grammar School in Victorian times.

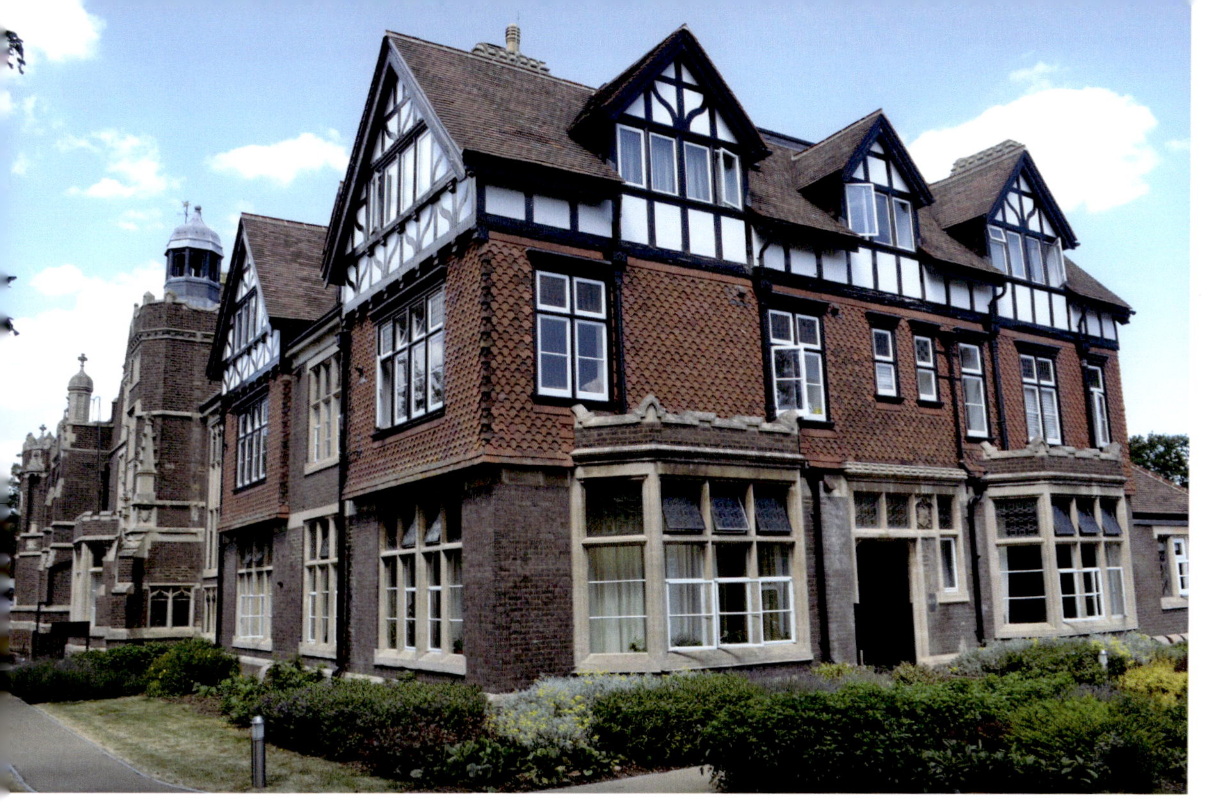

Above: The former Grammar School, one of the finest buildings in Dunstable.

Right: The old entrance to the school and its magnificent doorway.

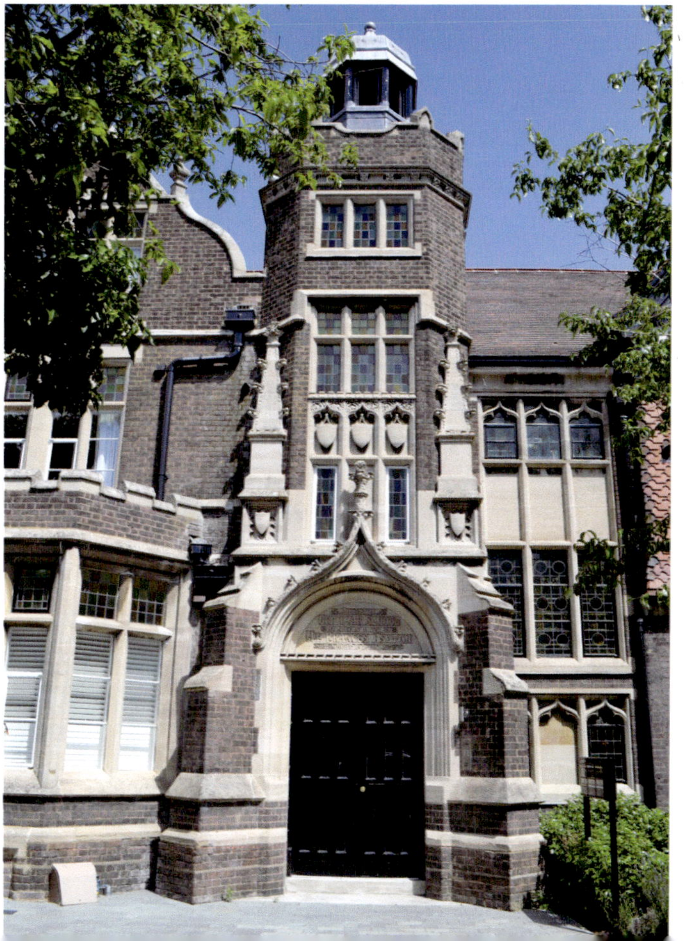

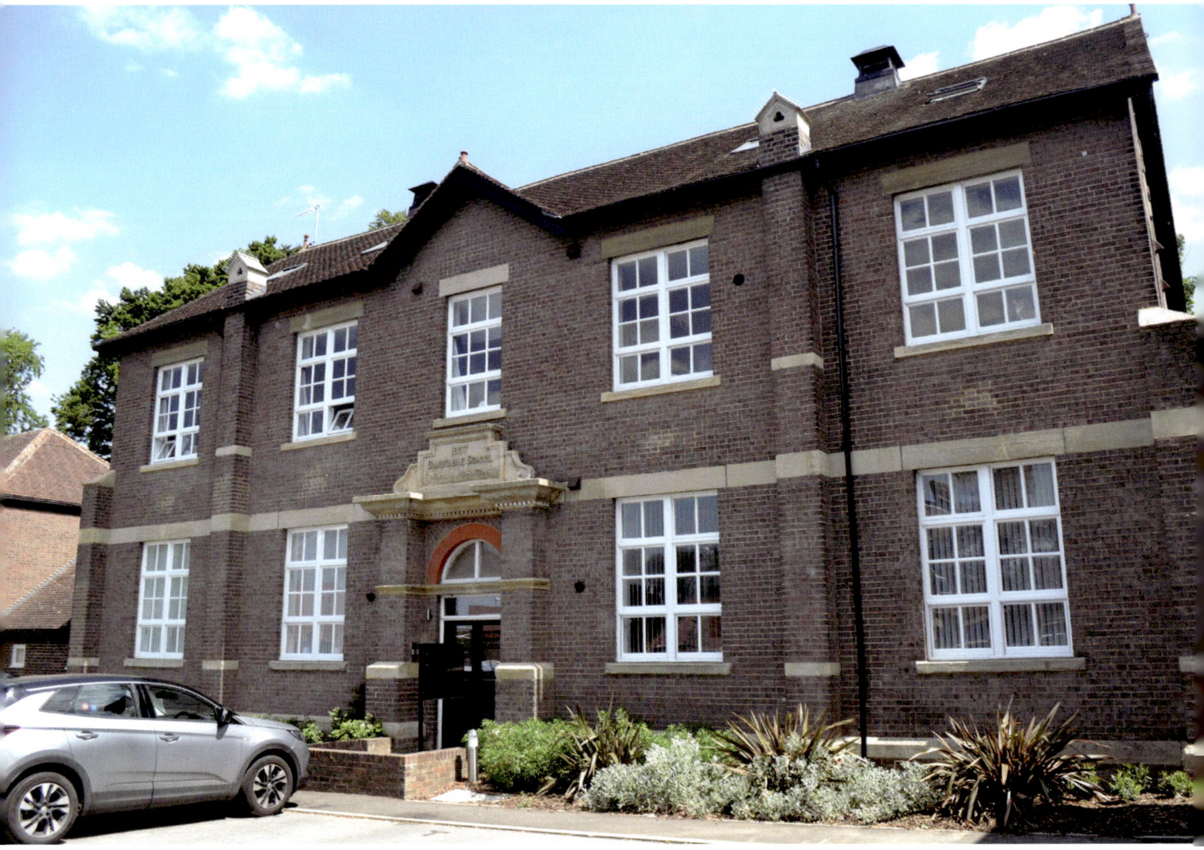

The science laboratories were added in 1907.

originally used as a playing field by the boys of Ashton Grammar School. On it stood an old windmill, which belonged to Mr F. Simmons.

The original grammar school building was modernised in 1973 and housed the Ashton Middle School, for children aged nine to thirteen, up until 2016 when it eventually closed. The buildings were then sold and converted to high-quality residential units.

25. The Former Police Station, Icknield Street

Dunstable Borough Police Force was established on 16 September 1865, when the council appointed just two men to keep law and order in the town. They were Head Constable Benjamin George (later superintendent) and PC Addington (promoted to sergeant in 1870). They were issued with uniforms consisting of 'one great coat and cape every two years and every year one body coat, two pairs of trousers, two pairs of boots and one hat'. Mr Burr gave the council a piece of

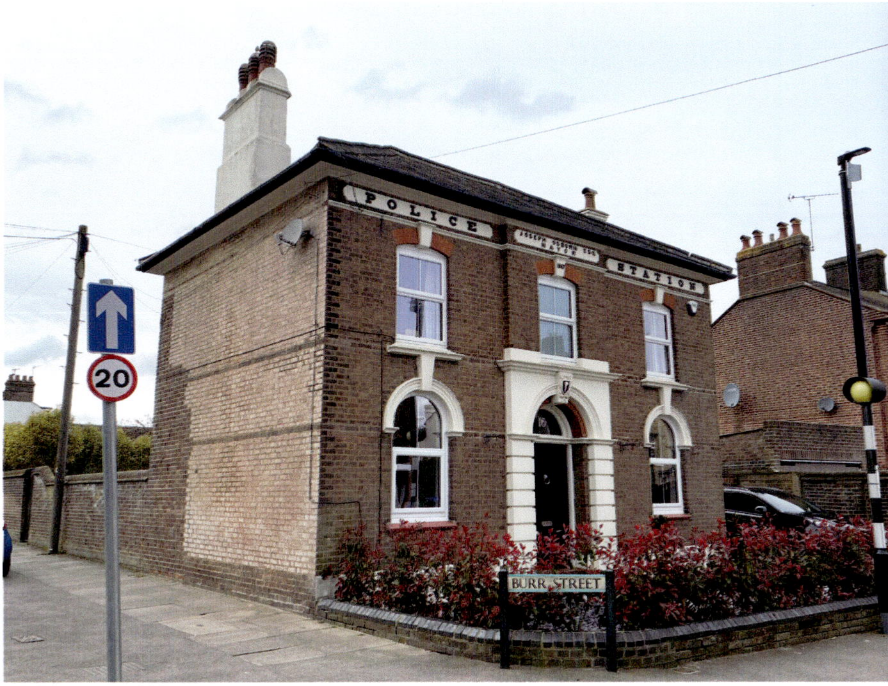

Right: The former police station on Icknield Street.

Below: A former use of this building clear for all to see.

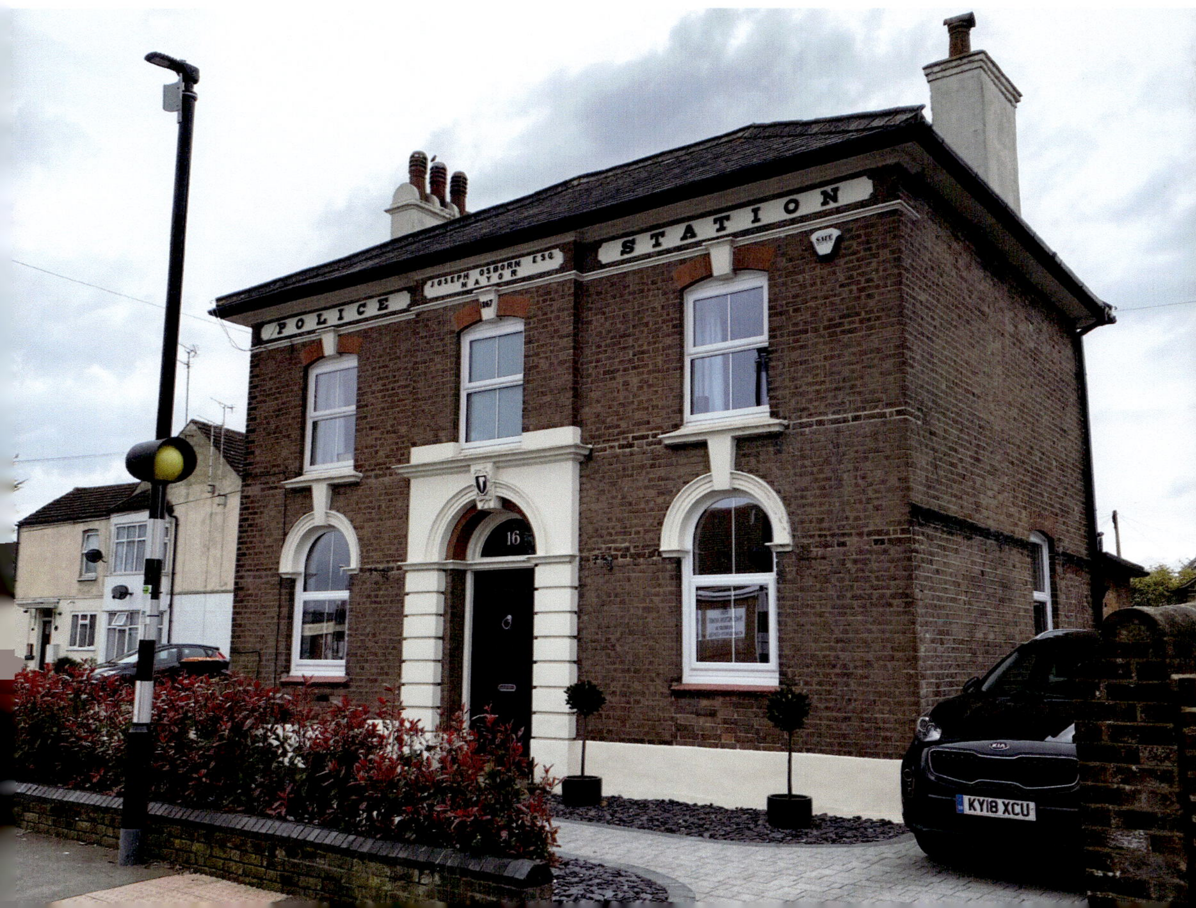

land, 'Butt's Field' in Icknield Street, on which the police station was built to the cost of £425. It opened in December when a second constable, William Prior, was appointed during the illness of Head Constable George. The following year PC Prior was considered too old for the job and replaced by Henry Tofield.

The new police station came about as the original lock-up was no longer deemed suitable, with complaints cited in May 1867 from Inspector of the Constabulary Lieutenant General Cartwright, who stated that 'it was not suitable for the detention of prisoners and that the minimum requirement was a lock-up with two cells and living accommodation for a constable'.

Today the building has been converted for residential use.

26. Polish Catholic Church, Victoria Street

The Polish Catholic Church in Victoria Street, or the Parish Church of Our Lady of Czestochowa, was originally a Methodist chapel built in 1862. The Methodists had been meeting from 1852 in a small chapel in Mount Street, at the corner of the lane leading from Edward Street to Princes Street. Earlier they had met in the bar of a disused pub, the Rising Sun, in Edward Street.

The Polish Catholic Church on Victoria Street.

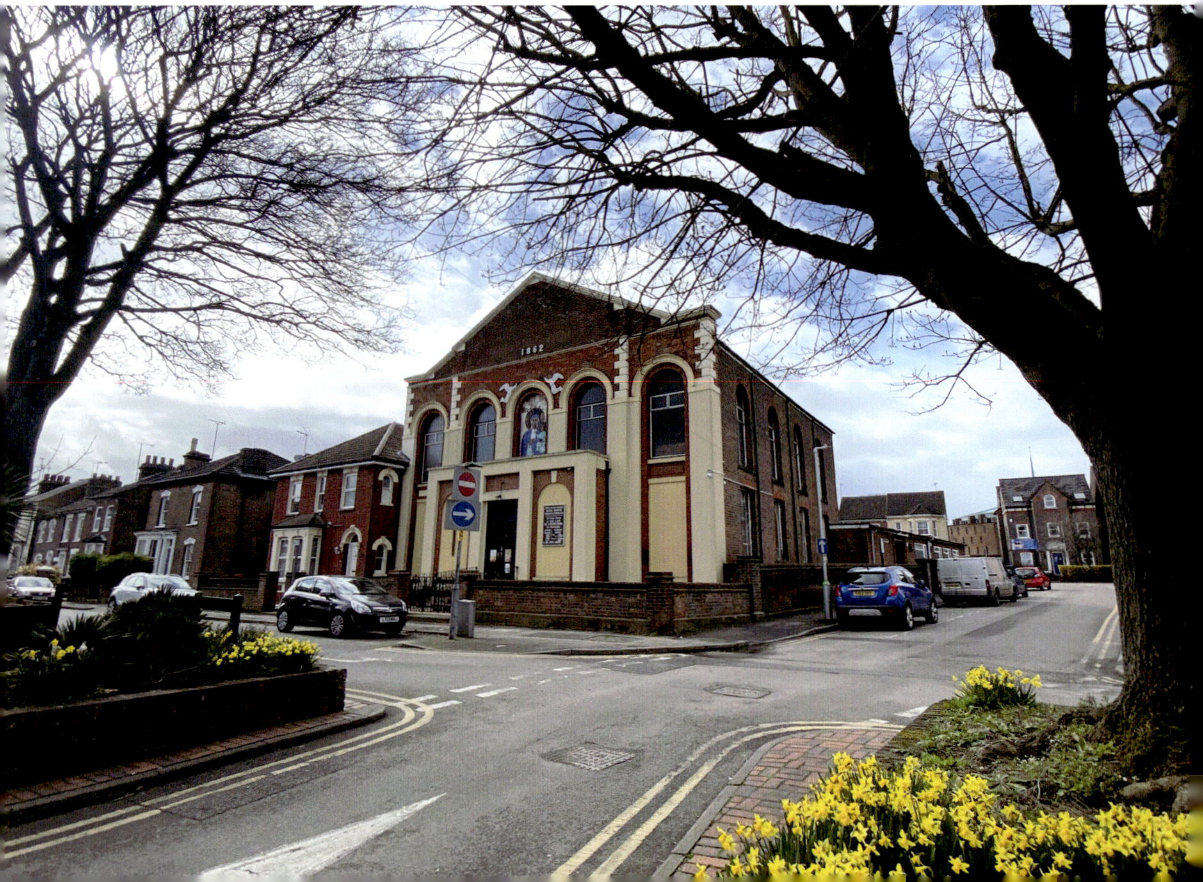

After the end of the Second World War many Polish soldiers, for personal or political reasons, decided not to return to Poland but to stay abroad. They took advantage of the invitation of the then British Foreign Minister to settle here. They were temporarily placed in post-military camps. One of them was in Marsworth, near Dunstable, and it was this camp that became the first nucleus of this parish.

One of the first priests who took care of this new and growing Polish community was Father Włodzimierz Cieński. He made contact with St Joseph's in Luton and received permission to celebrate Mass here in Polish. By 1953 this parish officially began to exist. The local Polish community, including many former Polish soldiers who had been unable to return to their homeland after the war, raised the money buy the chapel, then disused, and reopened in the building in 1968 as Our Lady of Czestochowa Catholic Church.

Life in the parish was by now booming. Many church and social organisations were gradually established that developed and grew under the leadership and care of successive parish priests. The parish now covers not only Luton and Dunstable and Milton Keynes, but also several nearby towns and villages.

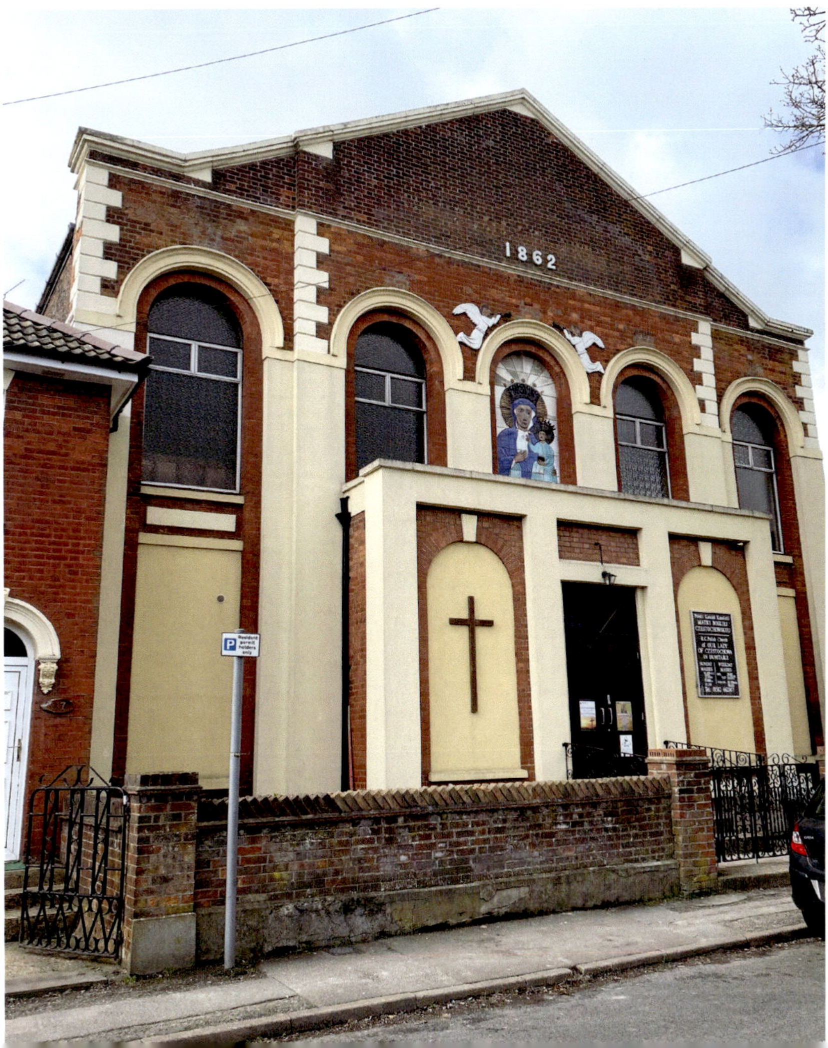

Colourful and unforgettable frontage of the Polish Catholic Church on Victoria Street.

27. Strict Baptist Chapel, St Mary's Gate

The first indirect reference to what is now Dunstable Baptist Church on St Mary's Gate is in a list of place names in the account of a Second General Meeting: 'At a meeting of chosen messengers of the churches at Wormsley, the 3rd day of the 9th month 1652, viz., of Abingdon, Reading, Henley, Kensworth, Eversholt etc.' There is no specific reference to Dunstable, but there is to Kensworth, the village on the Downs to the south of the town. It was here that during the earlier part of that century people used to gather in the open air to hear itinerant preachers, including Revd Edward Harrison. He was very impressed by these preachers, going out to hear them for himself. When the Civil War broke out, he joined the Parliamentary forces at Newport Pagnell as secretary and confidential messenger. In the late 1640s he became pastor of the Baptist church, meeting at Petty France in London. It is perhaps not surprising then that a church was formed at Kensworth. It is worth mentioning two important factors to bear in mind as the story of the church unfolds. Firstly, we are talking about a church that, by and large, was made up of very poor people. It is probably true to say that this was the case through practically all its history, up to the twentieth century. In the middle of the seventeenth century conditions were about the worst they have ever been for the poorest in society. Secondly, during the larger part of that century, those who came to believe what the members of the Kensworth church believed and practised were subject to official opposition and actual persecution.

The first records of the Kensworth church itself date from 1675. At that time members were scattered over a wide area around – from Mimms on the Middlesex border to St Albans, to Welwyn, Leighton Buzzard and Berkhamsted. Quite what this means is not certain. Separate churches are recorded at an earlier date in several of these places. It may be that these were considered to be congregations of the Kensworth church, or it may be that the troubled times for Nonconformists following the Restoration had resulted in the break up of churches. An out of the way village just inside the northern border of Hertfordshire was the very place where a church could survive. In any case, it is probable that the church did not meet very often for worship as one body, but that this took place in a number of centres led by someone local, with preachers visiting each group on occasions.

Worshippers were drawn from twenty-seven towns and villages, and only four of them actually lived in Kensworth. Where the church was located in Kensworth is unknown. There is no record of any church building, or meeting house, as it would have been called in those days, and it is extremely unlikely that there would have been one. In earlier times it suited the church to meet at Kensworth, but later when circumstances had changed it was more convenient to meet in Dunstable.

It was probably in the late 1640s that the Kensworth church was established, which would make it one of the earliest Baptist churches in the country. It was doubtless very convenient for people to meet away from Dunstable. Unauthorised religious meetings, or conventicles as they were called, were illegal, so to meet just over in Hertfordshire, out of the jurisdiction of the Bedfordshire magistrates, was a wise precaution.

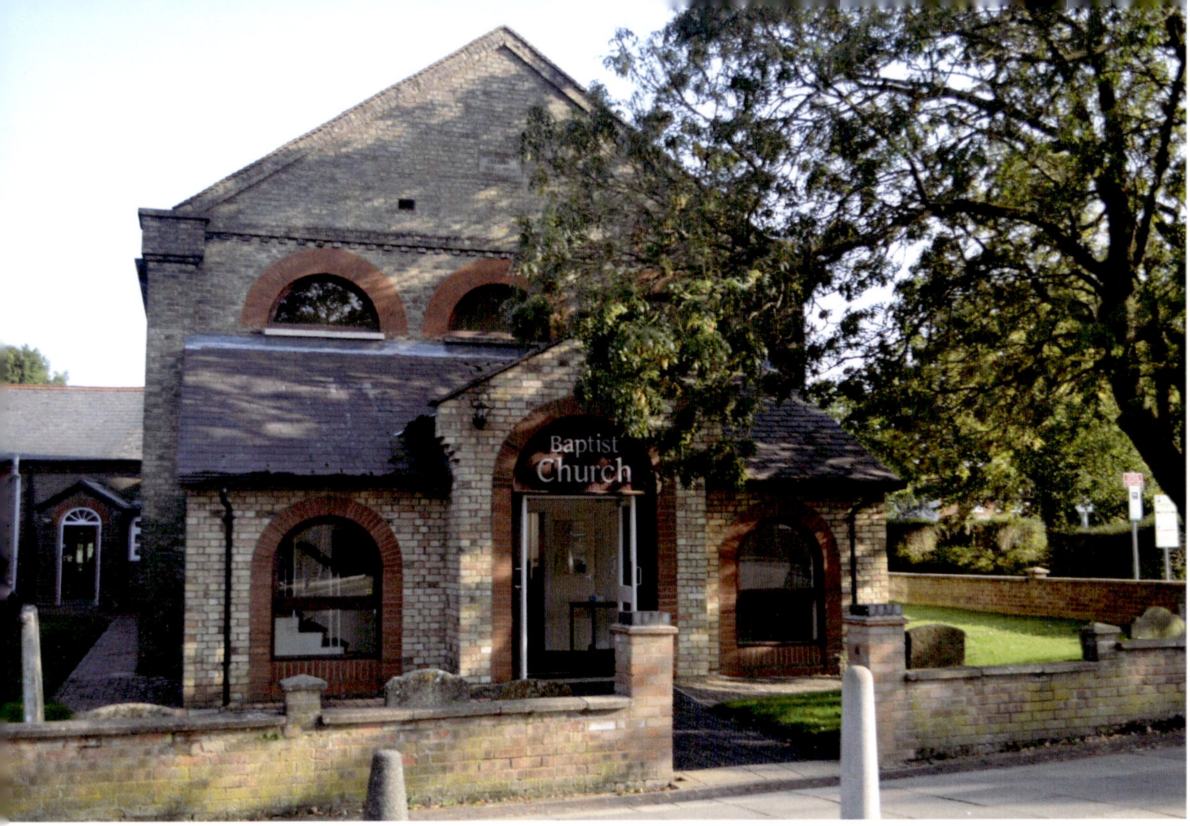

Above: The strict Baptist Chapel on St Mary's Gate.

Below: Rebuilt in 1849 but incorporating some of the older building.

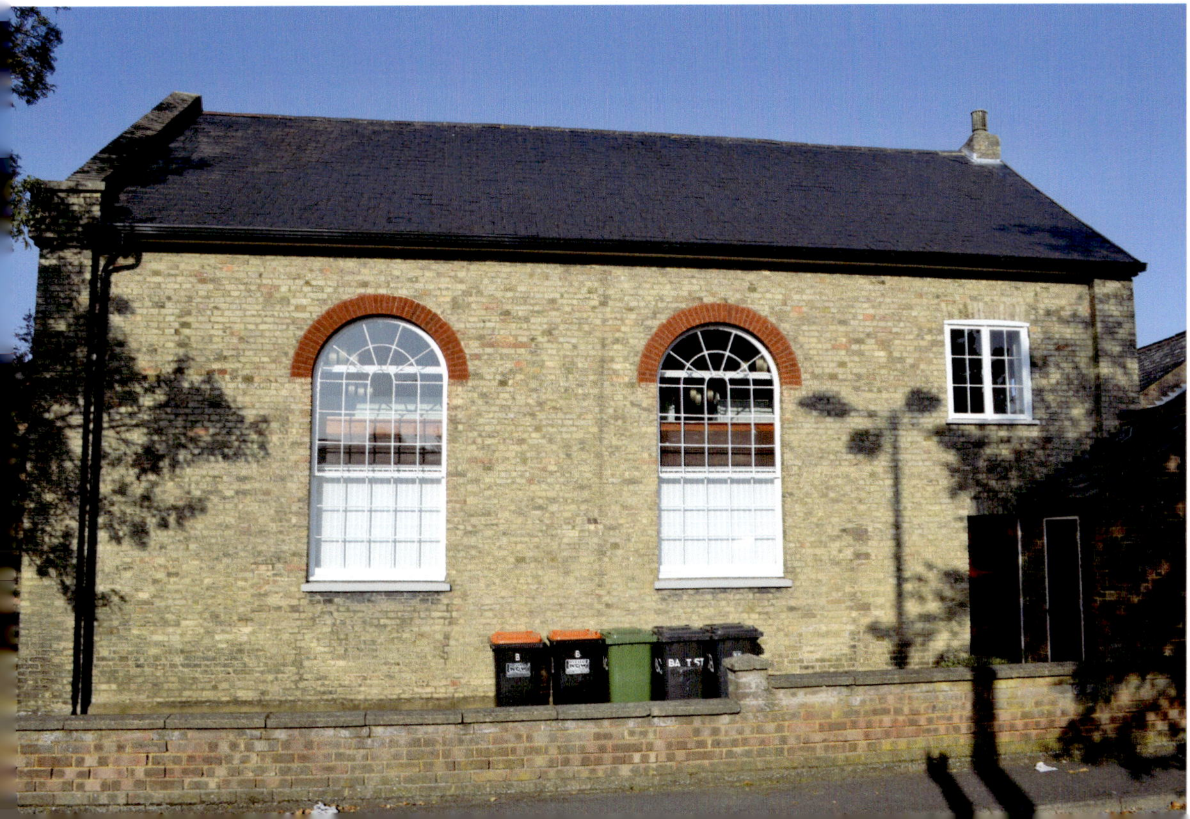

The first meeting house was eventually built in Dunstable in 1708. The record reads: 'In the year 1708 built then an house at Dunstable for the public worship of God – The ground cost ten pounds. The writings cost two pounds. The charge for stuff and workmanship eighty and one pounds and two pence. The cost in all ninety three pounds and two pence. The writings belonging to the house are lodged in Brother Britten's hands.' There is a possibility that this meeting house was enlarged in 1807. It was rebuilt in 1849 when the present chapel was erected on the same site, apparently incorporating some part of the old building. Early on in that year a violent storm one Sunday afternoon damaged the roof, which fell in and endangered the lives of the worshippers. This building now has a vestibule, which was added to it a few years ago, and has been completely changed inside, with the old box pews having been removed and replaced by more comfortable chairs.

28. The Former Baptist Chapel, West Street

The joy of exploring towns and cities are the surprises that appear around a corner or hidden on some nondescript street. This can be said for this wonderful building. The former Baptist Church in West Street, Dunstable, opened for worship in June 1848. Its history can be traced back to a tiny Baptist meeting house in the hamlet of Thorn, near Houghton Regis, which was originally an offshoot of the Park Street Church in Luton but became a distinct church with its own ministers in June 1751. At one stage the building at Thorn was dismantled and lovingly re-erected at Houghton. In 1836 its Dunstable members decided to form their own church under Revd Daniel Gould, who had been pastor at Houghton since 1826 and was to continue at West Street until 1881. The church was founded by General Baptists as distinguished from the Particular or Strict Baptists at the Old Chapel in St Mary's Gate.

The building present today was built under the supervision of J. Clarke and was a red-brick church with decorative yellow-brick cornerstones and tall, arched windows. The original Dunstable meeting house was built in 1790 on a piece of land given by Mr R. Gutteridge adjacent to the present West Street site. The small Dunstable building had became too small and overcrowded and its condition deteriorated, so the new church was built to replace it, and was designed to seat 700 worshippers. In front of the church was a burial ground, but the gravestones were moved in around 1945, with a number of them used for pavings and some erected in an adjacent area to the east of the building. Members of the Chamber, Batchelor, Gutteridge and Osborn families were buried here. In February 1976, a new hall was built at the church as a cost of £38,000. In 1984, the front extension was added and the church was opened as a day school – the Pilgrims' Christian School of the New Covenant Church.

The building has retained its religious use and is an evangelical church in 2023, serving the needs of the Dunstable community and beyond.

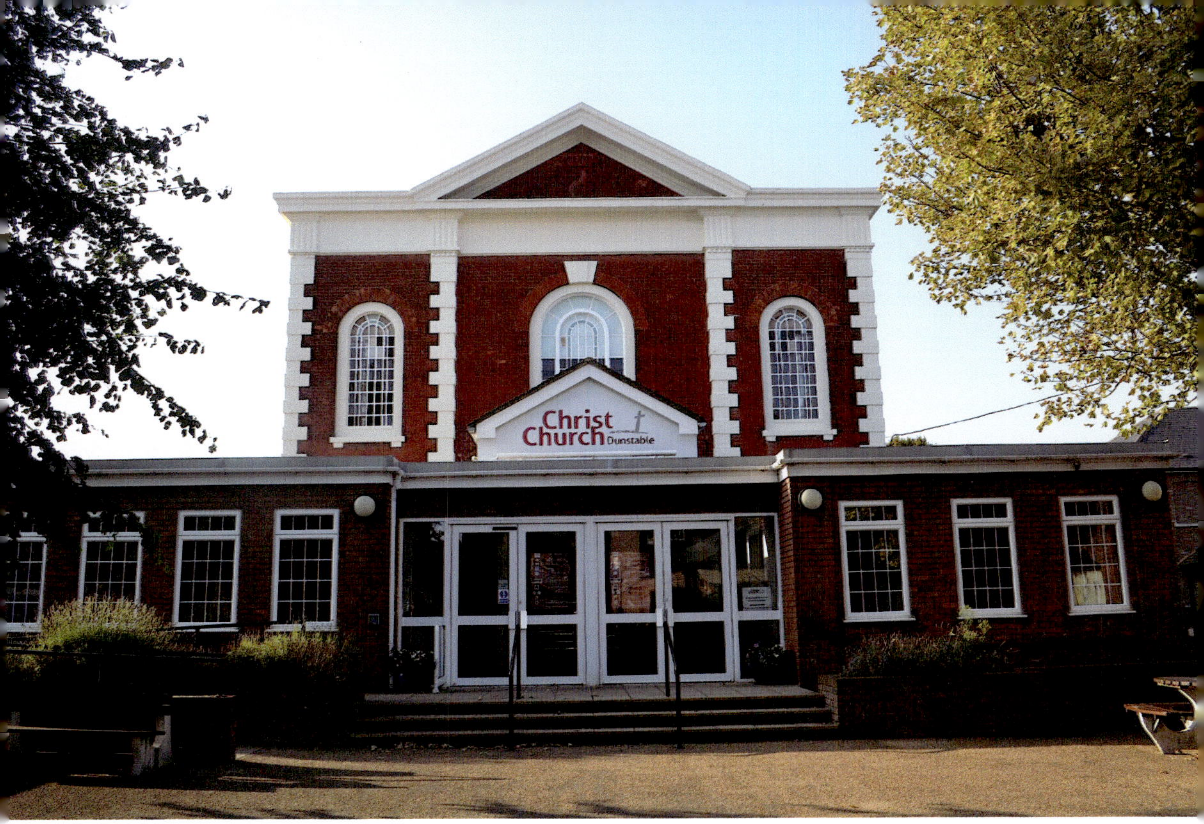

Above: The former Baptist Chapel, hidden off West Street.

Below: The side and rear of the Baptist Chapel off West Street, a substantial building.

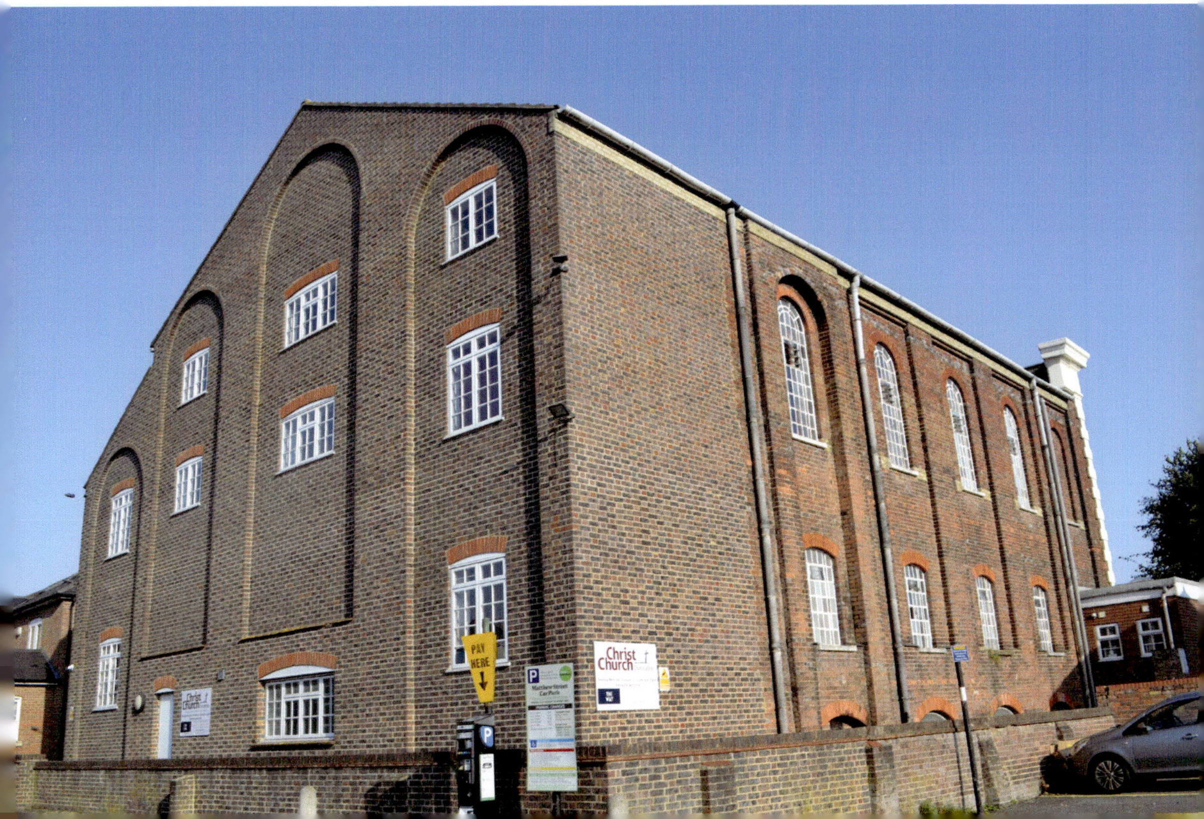

29. The Little Theatre, High Street South

Built in 1883, the current Little Theatre was originally an extension of the adjacent Chew's School, by the trustees of the Chew's Funds. The building was therefore constructed with large windows to light up the school classrooms. After the school closed this building was taken over in October 1938 by the Dunstable branch of the Bedfordshire County Library. The library before this had been housed in the old town hall between 1925 and 1927, then in the Kingsbury Barn between 1927 and 1934 along with the Dunstable Museum.

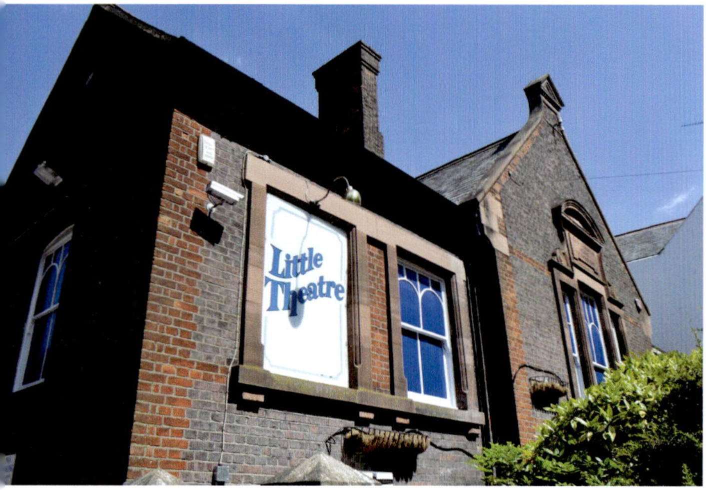

Left: The Little Theatre, once the town's library.

Below: Large windows that let in ample light, now closed off for its theatrical use.

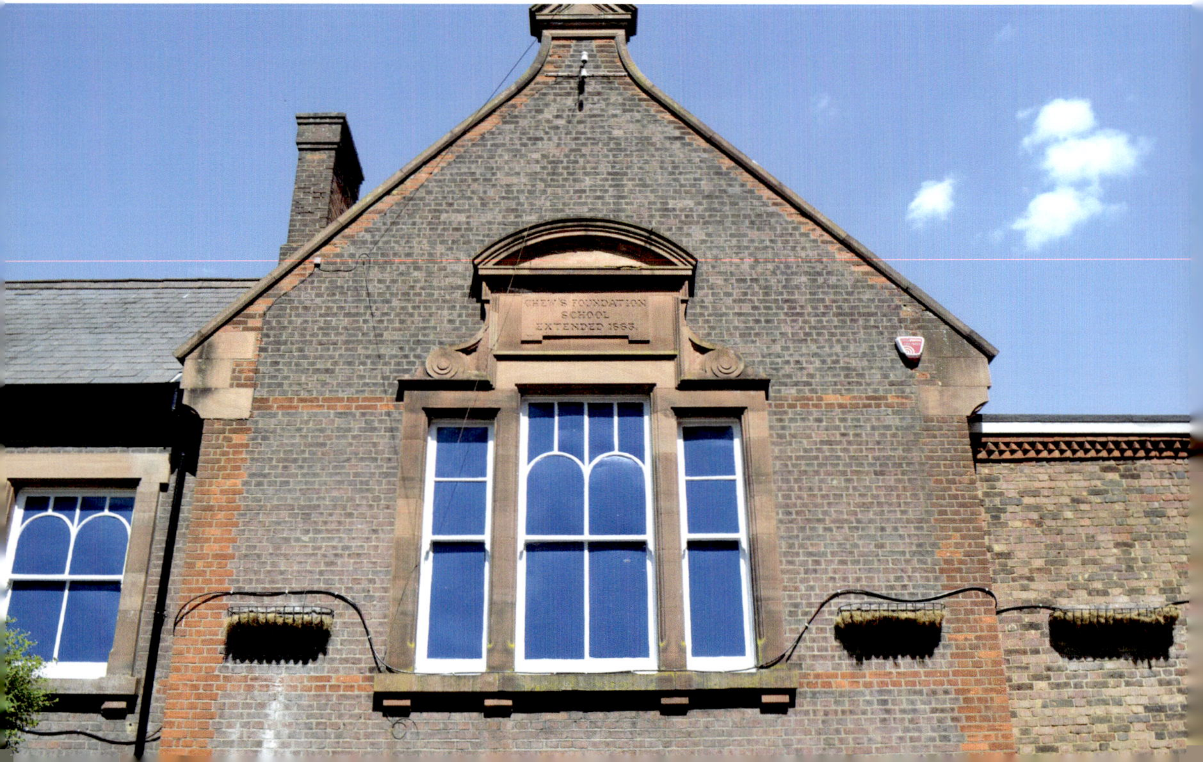

The building lent itself for use as a library, with the large windows allowing in plenty of light and the figured oak panelling giving the building a distinguished appearance. The library was popular and very well stocked; it had a children's corner called Lilliput Library because of its very small chairs and tables. The library was here until the 1960s when it moved to new premises in the Quadrant.

Once the library had left, the building was taken over by the Dunstable Repertory Company, who had previously used the old town hall. The large windows were all boarded up and the interior was converted into a small theatre, which was officially opened in October 1968 as The Little Theatre by actor Bernard Bresslaw.

30. No. 52 High Street South, Former Hat Factory Manager's House

A reminder of the straw hat industry in Dunstable is found at No. 52 High Street South on the Square, opposite Priory Gate. This late eighteenth-century building was once the hat factory manager's house attached to Stuart, Sons and Co.'s straw

A former hat factory manager's house, a reminder of the town's association with the hat industry.

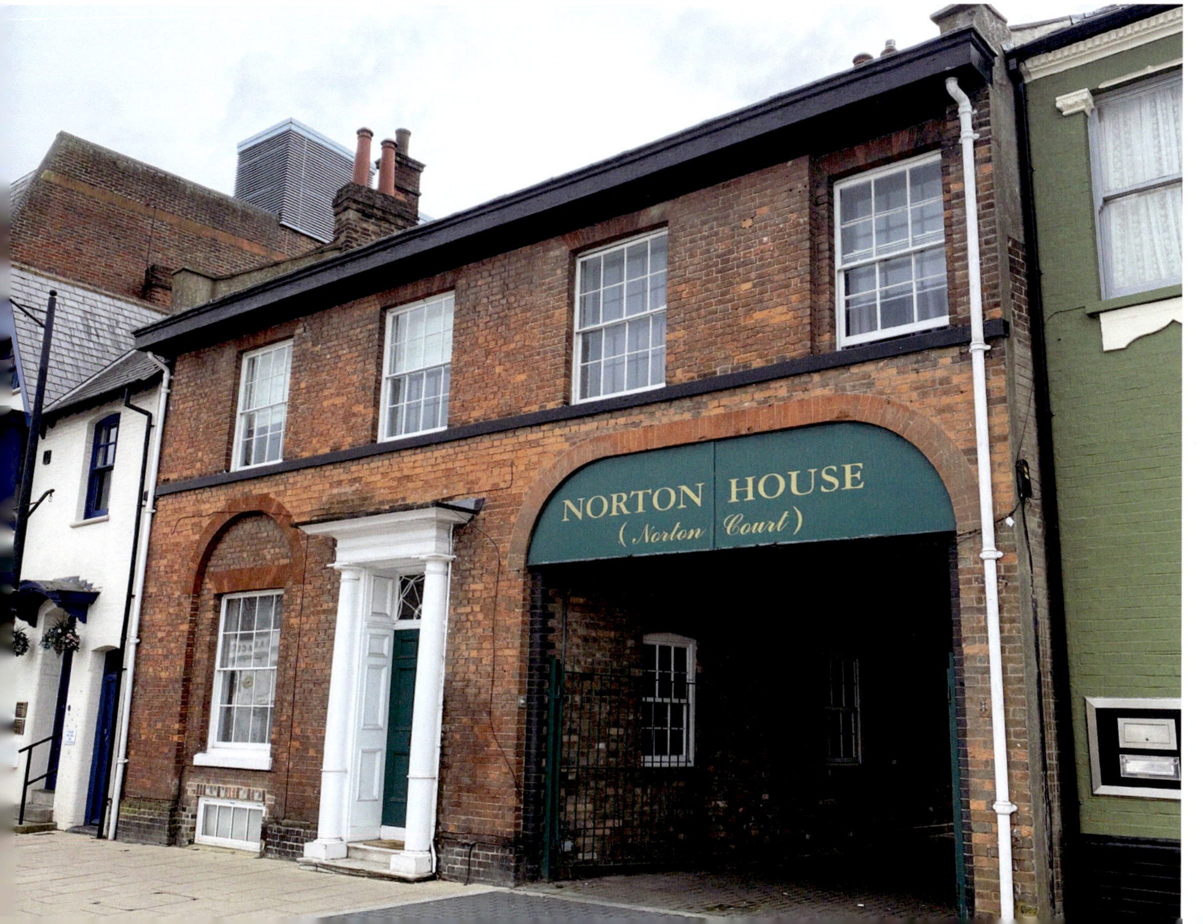

hat factory. The business had been present in Dunstable for many years when it closed down in 1924, making it one of the last hat factories in the town. The last one finally closed a few years later in 1931. In 1926, alterations were made to this building when it was converted from a hat factory into business premises.

31. Dunstable Cemetery

By the 1830s Priory Churchyard had become too small for the town, so a new cemetery was planned to meet the needs of a growing population. After much initial opposition to the idea of a new cemetery (the vicar thought that the churchyard could cope for another 200 years), it eventually found favour. A committee of thirteen people representing different denominations within the town was then elected in 1860 with a view to purchasing land and buildings. A site on West Street was considered the most suitable for a new cemetery, and enough land was purchased for the surplus to be rented out for grazing until it was needed. Designs for two chapel buildings connected by an arch, together with two lodges and ornamental gates, were submitted by Luton architect George Halton. These were approved by the committee in July 1861 and tenders for the building work were sought.

This beautiful building is substantially the same today, although the large ornamentation on the roof above the archway has been removed, as well as the crucifixes above the chapels and the ornamental gates. There are large trees along

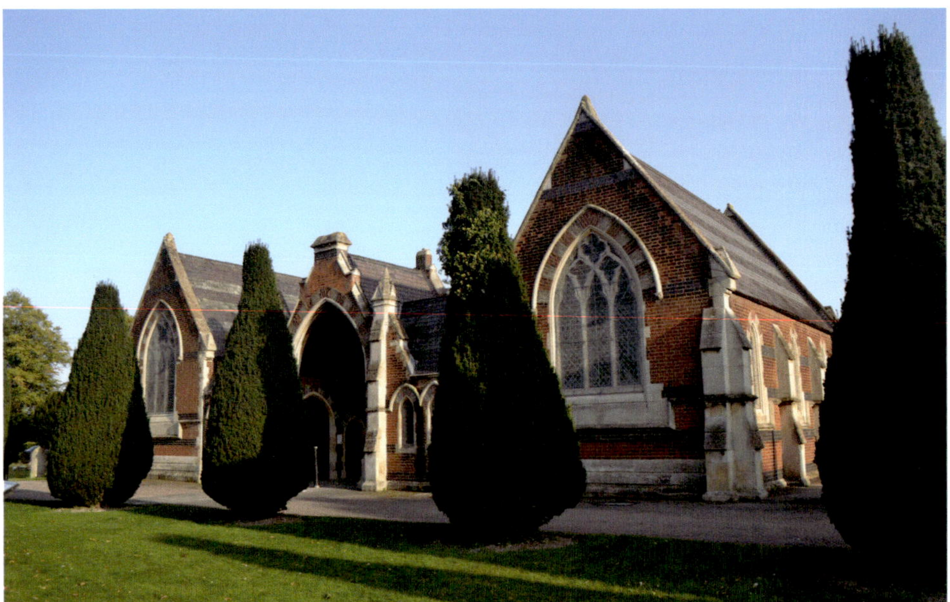

Dunstable Cemetery entrance buildings.

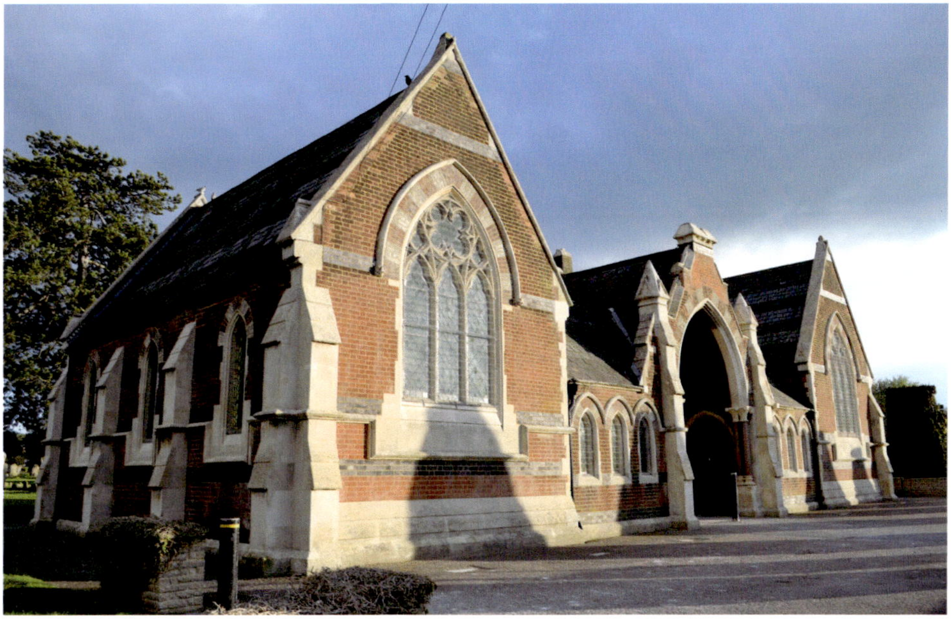

Above: The main entrance buildings to Dunstable Cemetery, which was consecrated in 1864.

Right: The fine Gothic-style arch to Dunstable Cemetery.

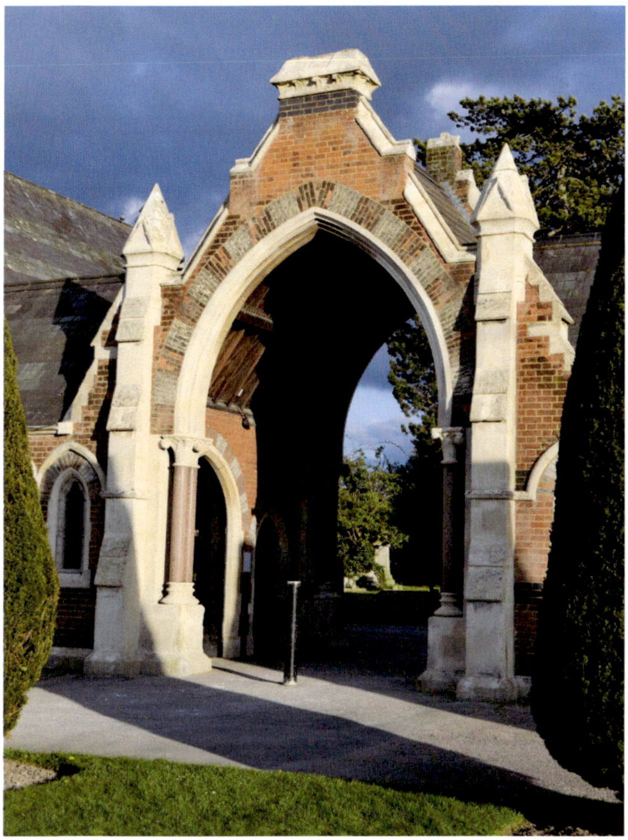

much of the frontage now and the old lodge house on the left of the entrance, which provided accommodation for the cemetery manager, has been demolished. The chapel on the right-hand side remains. The cemetery was consecrated on Friday 19 August 1864 by the Bishop of Ely, Dr Harold Browne, with prayers and lessons read by the rector of Priory Church, Revd Frederick Hose.

The first interment at the cemetery tells a sad tale and took place on 22 October 1861, when James Turney, aged just four, was buried. James was the son of Thomas and his wife Eliza who lived in Church Street. On the 1861 census return, Thomas is shown as an omnibus driver (horse-driven at this time). The death certificate shows he died on 20 October 1861 of acute hydrocephalus.

32. The Globe Public House

This excellent example of a nineteenth-century public house has changed little on the exterior of the building, although internal changes have been considerable. The name of the pub was first advertised in 1876 when Joseph Fearn was occupying The Globe as a victualler and cooper. He moved here in about 1871, having previously been at the Crow (eventually the Crown Inn). By 1885, Henry North was at The Globe, followed by Francis Ashplant (1894). At the beginning of the twentieth century Patrick Kelly was landlord (1903, 1914) followed by Frederick Kelly (1920) and Mrs Kelly (1921). By 1924, The Globe was occupied by Robert George King, who had moved from the Rifle Volunteers. It is still a popular pub to this day.

The Globe, still serving drinks today.

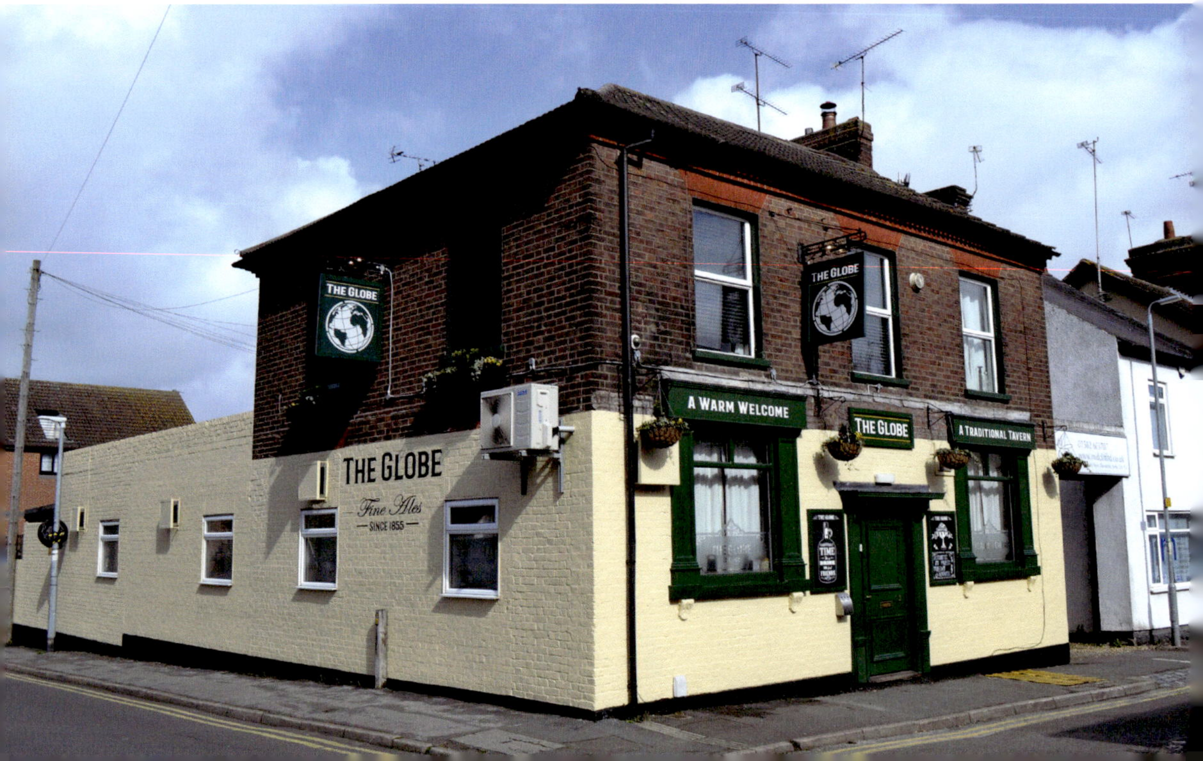

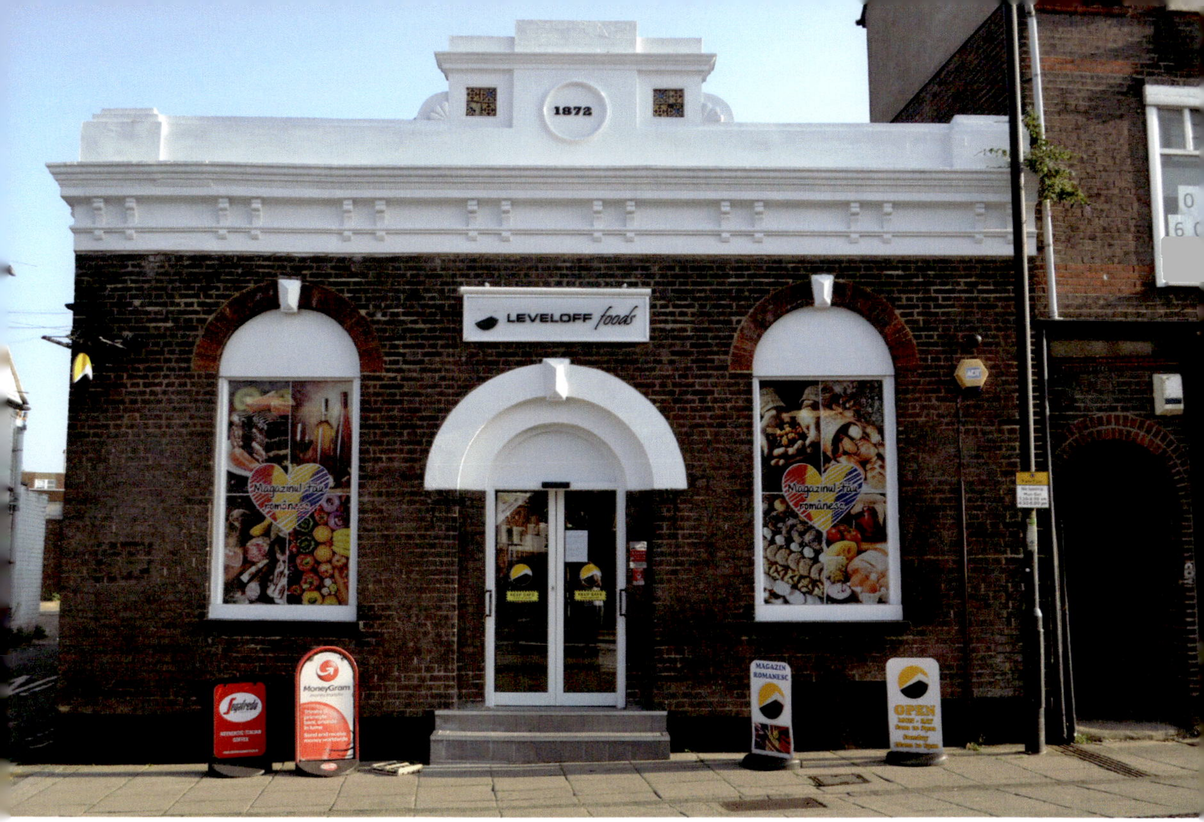

Once a popular bookshop, now a mini supermarket.

33. Former Book Castle, Church Street

There is no missing the date of this quirky building on Church Street, as it sits above the main door. It dates from 1872 and was used as a drill hall by local volunteer soldiers for many years. It became The Book Castle bookshop, taking its name from the architectural design of its frontage, hinting at military fortification. The Book Castle published a number of local history books including *Dunstable in Detail* by Nigel C. Benson in 1986, a primary source of information for this book. Today it is a specialist mini-supermarket.

34. The Crown Inn

One of the many public houses on High Street North is the Crown. During the nineteenth century it was known as the Crow, and may well have also been known as the Raven at one time. Crows have been associated with Dunstable for many years with the saying 'as black as a Dunstable crow'. There have also been rumours that crows were trained to carry letters before pigeons were used, but this is likely to be a local myth. In the nineteenth century, the curiously named Francis Ratt was the landlord at the Crow for a number of years, but by 1870 it had changed its name to the Crown Inn. Further up High Street North used to be a well-known coaching inn called the Crown, which became a hat factory in 1847. The owners of the Crow wished to capitalise on the reputation of the former Crown Inn, so it was used to replace the old Crow's name.

The 1871 census records the inn as the Crown with Frederick Field as the landlord. By 1894 and several landlords later, George Pleasant had taken over and was landlord for many years until after 1924. By 1928, William Hill was running the Crown and also stayed for many years. The pub remained popular for a number of decades, but, as with many recent public houses, in 2023 its future remained in doubt and its doors were closed for business.

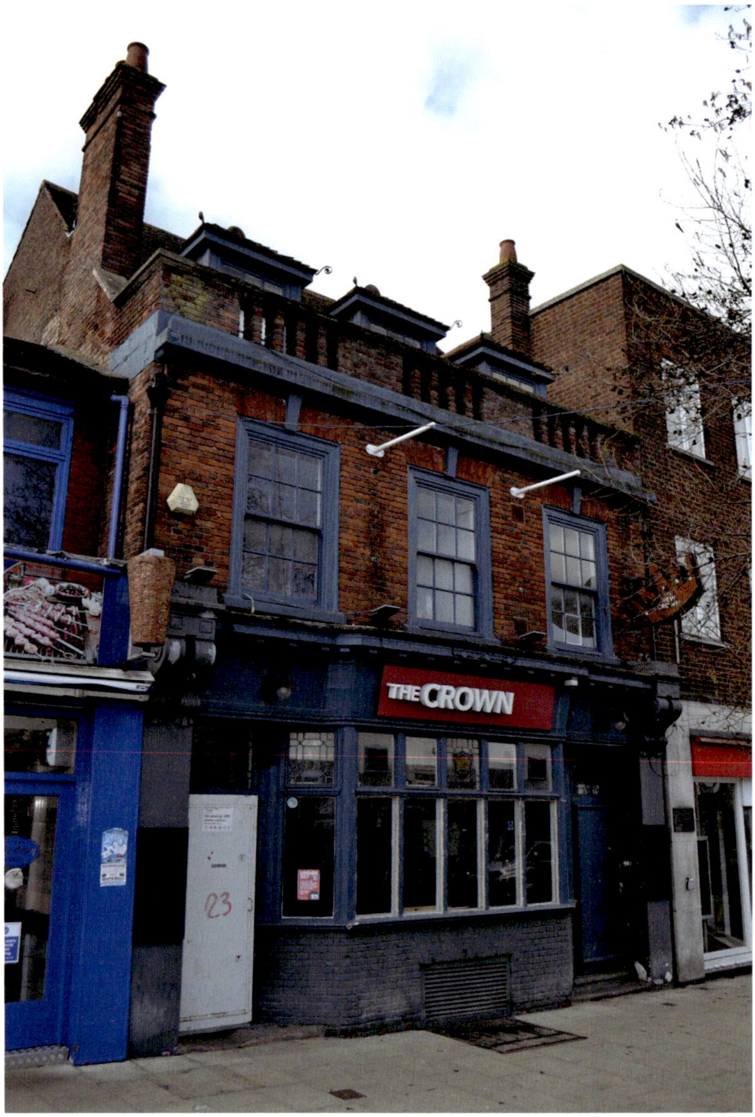

The Crown Inn, closed for business in 2023.

35. Chiltern House, High Street North

On High Street North and on the corner of Regent Street is the rather subdued but magnificent Chiltern House. The majority of local history books and guided trails seem to ignore this forlorn and seemingly forgotten building, despite its Grade II listing. It was built in the early to mid-nineteenth century with a plumb-coloured brick. It was originally the home of William Paxton Reading Southam, who is described in Kelly's Directory of 1894 as 'auctioneer and registrar of marriages for Luton District, Regent Street'. It then became the family home of William Lockhart, coal merchant and builders merchant. The Lockharts were well known in Dunstable for many years.

Charles Lockhart (1817–92) established his business at Nos 3 and 4 High Street South in 1840 and lived above his shop with his wife and eleven children. It was probably the largest shop in the town and went through to Church Street. He was not only a 'Draper and Silk Mercer', but his shop also had a large furniture department. His son Charles was later involved in the family business. Lockhart and Son also became funeral directors, hiring out Shillibeer mourning carriages with black horses. They also had a large trade in mourning wear.

The 1871 census also shows Charles and his wife, Elizabeth, living above the shop with some of their children: Arthur (who was 'afflicted with epilepsy'), Emma Elizabeth and William Henry, who became a Wesleyan minister.

Lockhart's had many customers in the surrounding villages. They also ran a club and in the autumn the villagers would be brought in by wagonette to spend their club money. A year's worth of paying into the club would earn the customer a bonus of 3*s* in the pound.

By 1891 Charles had handed over the running of his business to his son Charles, and he and Elizabeth were living at North House, next to Mr and Mrs Brown of Park Farm in High Street North. Charles is described as 'Gent and JP' in the census of that year. Charles and his wife both died during the 1890s. Charles Jr and his wife, Sarah Sophia, also had a large family. The 1881 census shows him and his family living above the shop with seven children: Neville, Ellie, Hilda, Mabel, Olive, George and Melville. In later years the first shop was taken over by Foster Brothers, which sold men's and boys' clothing, and Percy Ashwell was next door selling ladies' wear.

Mr Ashwell's business had originally been at No. 1, but he sold it to Home and Colonial and by 1917 he had moved to Lockhart's former premises. The last of the Lockhart family, Charles's son Melville, worked for Percy Ashwell for many years. Melville Scott Lockhart is described by Fred Moore as 'one of the old school, always formally dressed in black coat, grey waistcoat, striped trousers, and of great integrity'. He served in the Royal Army Medical Corps and won several decorations for gallantry. Mr Ashwell later sold his shop to Gibbs and Dandy.

Further down High Street South, on land once owned by Thomas Crawley of Priory House, was a red-brick dwelling house owned by the Taylor family since 1744. In 1851 it was bought by Edward Lockhart, who named it 'Lanark House'. This was No. 17 High Street South, next to Priory House.

Edward Lockhart (1808–78) was married in 1830 to Elizabeth Sarah Gostelow. The Gostelows were a prominent local family. In 1848 Edward started a coal sales business at the newly opened Dunstable North railway station. The 1851 census shows Edward and Elizabeth living in the High Street with their family: George, Elizabeth, Mary Ann, Walter, Alfred, Harriet, Eliza and William. The couple had two other sons, Edward and Thomas, not present during census night. Edward is described as 'Agent to coal merchant', with his son George as his assistant.

By 1861 he is listed as a coal and salt merchant and the 1871 census shows him as 'JP, Church Warden, Guardian and Coal Merchant'. Like Charles Lockhart, Edward had become an important part of the Dunstable community, and he was mayor on three occasions in the 1870s. Charles and Edward were both listed as borough magistrates in 1876.

Some of Edward's sons moved to nearby towns and continued the family coal business. Edward's son William took over the Dunstable business and William's son Percy William served as town mayor in 1928–29. He was also a coal and builders merchant and lived at Cordova in West Street, more recently the home of Dunstable Old People's Welfare Association.

After Edward's death the Lockhart family home was leased to the Dunstable Medical Centre. In the 1920s it was again a private house, occupied by Mr Albert Norman Gutteridge and was later taken over by the Room family. The ground floor was converted into a women's fashion shop, run by Mrs Room, an

Chiltern House, once the home of the Lockharts of Dunstable.

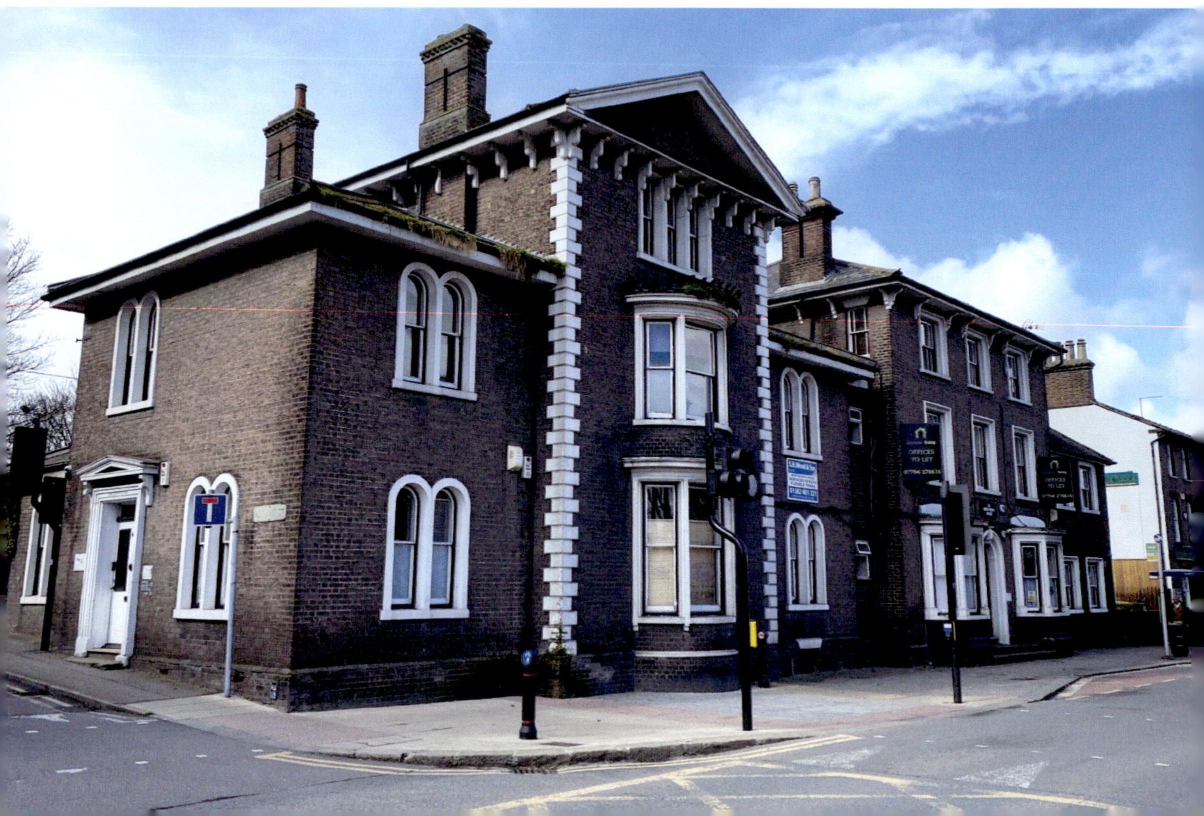

accomplished dressmaker. After Mrs Room retired, Mr and Mrs H. Mead took over the property and, from around 1940, ran it as the popular Priory Café.

The Dunstable Trade Directory for 1864 lists a third Lockhart – Henry. Henry Lockhart (1811–72) was a licensed victualler. In 1853 he occupied the Crown in Albion Street as a 'beer retailer and coach proprietor'. By 1863 he had moved on to the Red Lion Hotel on the corner of High Street North and Church Street. Henry and his wife Sarah do not appear to have had any children. The 1861 census shows Henry and Sarah living at the Red Lion with their twelve-year-old nephew, Abraham. When Abraham married, he went to live with his wife's family in Staffordshire.

In 1968 a new local road was named Lockhart Close in recognition of the Lockharts, who had been so prominent in the commercial life of the town. Glenn and Lyle Dentists were also here, with their infamous surgery downstairs and Mr and Mrs Glenn living above it with their three children. Many locals still have painful memories of visits to their surgery. Sadly, it is today another building in the town seeking a new future.

36. The Albion Buildings

Built in the nineteenth century, the Albion Buildings have had numerous occupants over many decades. In 1894, the International Tea Company's Stores

Albion Buildings.

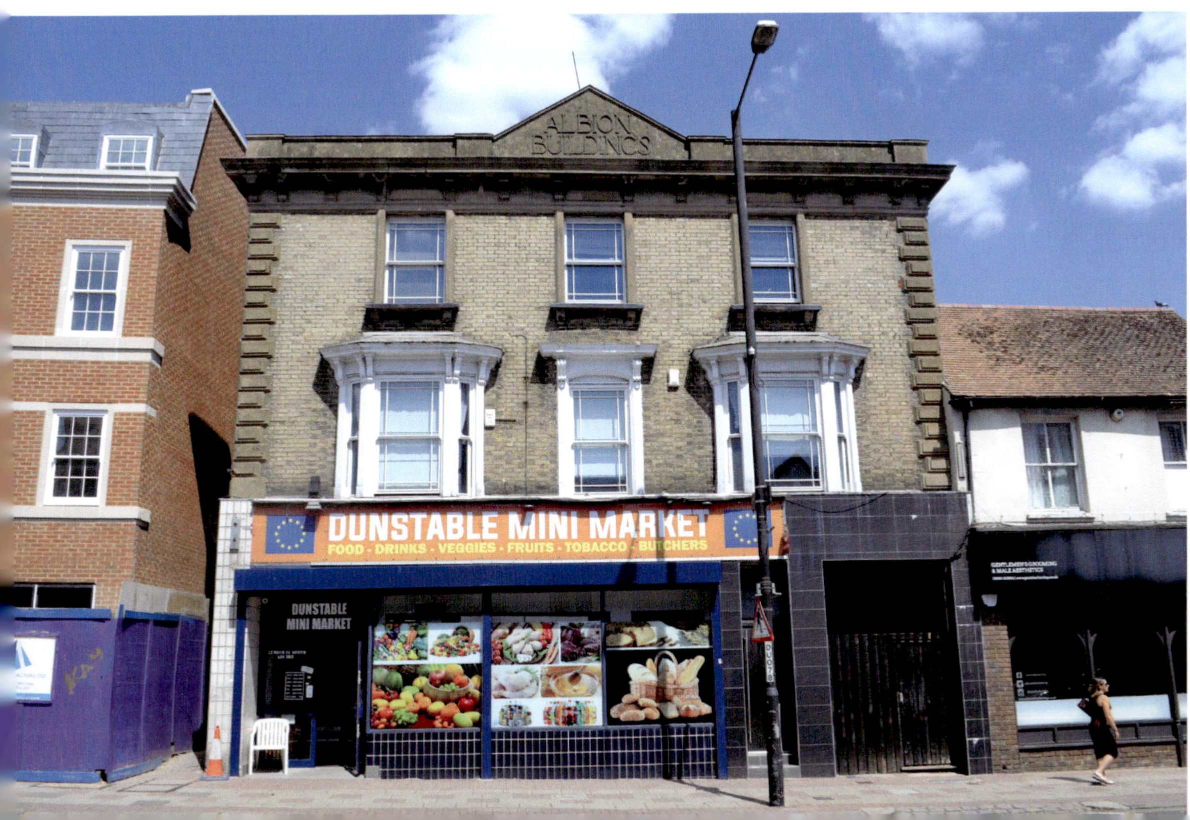

Ltd was at No. 2 Albion Buildings, with No. 1 Albion Buildings being occupied by the ironmonger's shop of William Francis. Old photographs at the end of the nineteenth century show many wares from the shop that were displayed on the pavement outside and baskets hanging on a gas street lamp at the end of Church Alley. A large sign above the shop advertised the vast range of items available, including 'Furniture and Ironmongery'. Many items were delivered to the premises by a horse and four-wheeled cart, which was often conveniently tied to the lamppost. The building here is an excellent example of why those who appreciate finer architecture should raise their eyes upwards.

37. The Former Wesleyan Chapel, High Street North

John Wesley (1703–91) visited Dunstable in 1758. His journal records that the weather that day was very unkind, as 'the rain continued all the way to Dunstable'. It is not recorded that he preached here that day but he certainly did, in nearby Luton and Sundon, and he had many followers in the town.

The former chapel on High Street North was built when Waterlows, the printers, came to Dunstable. This part of the town was developed by the British Land Company to accommodate print workers who moved with Waterlow and Sons from

A reminder of a religious and industrial past, this former Wesleyan chapel is now residential.

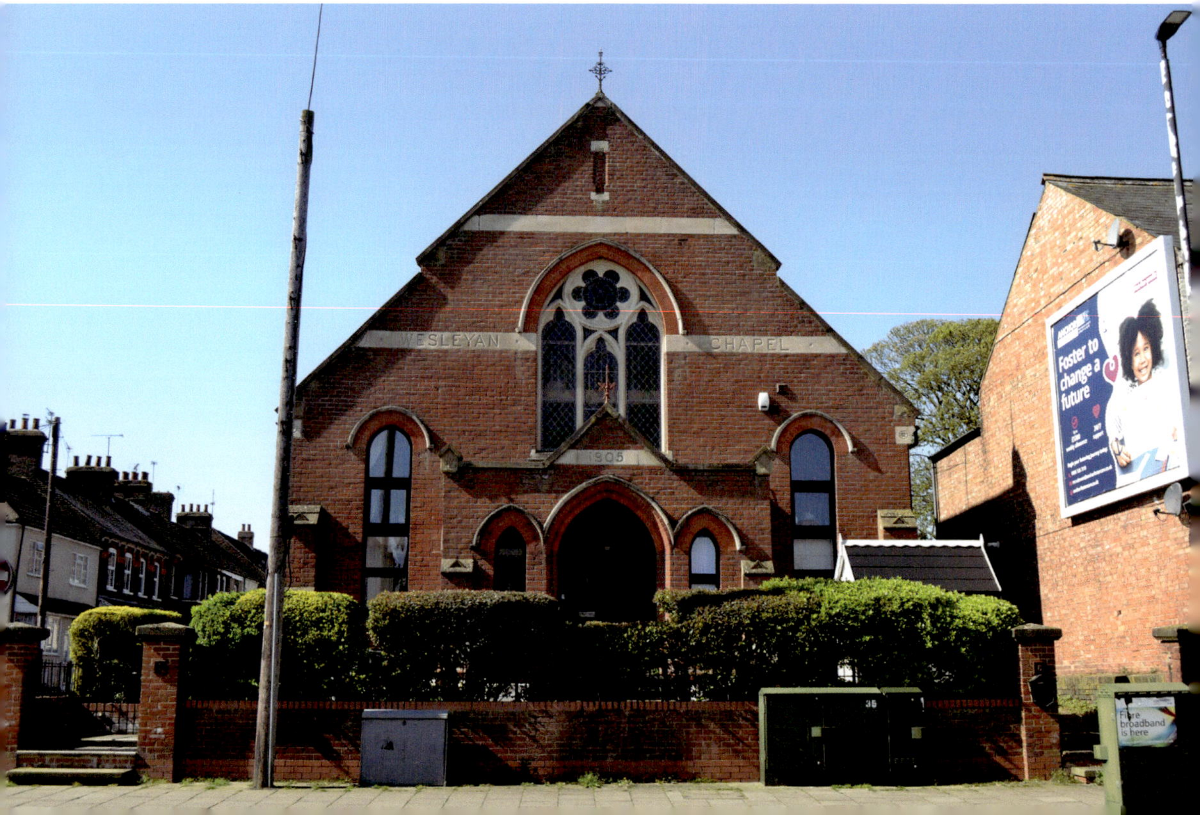

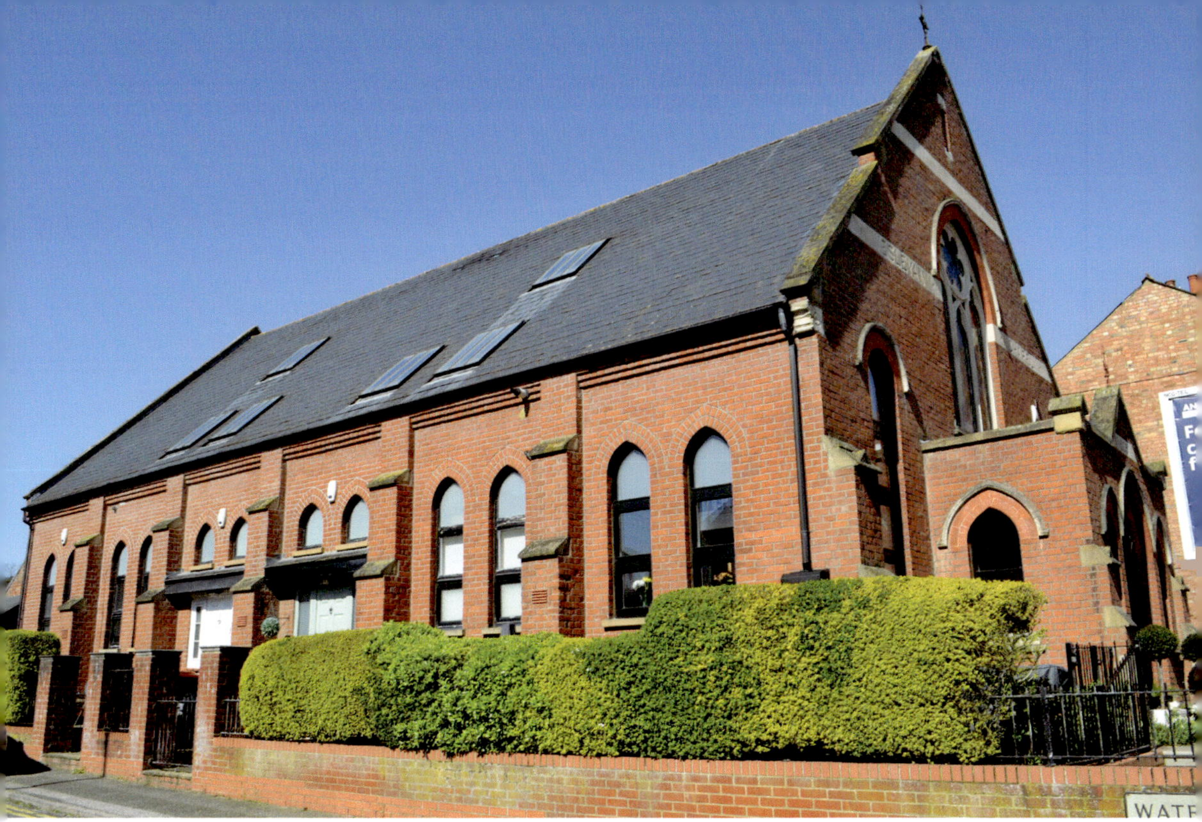

An excellent example of a historic building preserved, despite its change of use.

London in 1891. They built houses for the workers in nearby streets and a Wesleyan Chapel was provided for their spiritual needs. Situated on the corner of Waterlow Road and High Street North, it displays a 1905 date stone. The chapel here was in use up until 1998 and was eventually converted into apartments in 2001.

38. Methodist Church, the Square

Methodists in Dunstable owe their origins to a local carpenter and joiner called John Darley. Darley had heard of the great John Wesley, the founder of Methodism, and on a visit to Nottingham in 1770 he travelled to the nearby small market town of Bingham, Nottinghamshire, to hear Wesley preach. In his journal dated 30 July, Wesley was characteristically blunt about the occasion: 'I preached at Bingham, ten miles from Nottingham. I really admired the exquisite stupidity of the people. They gaped and stared while I was speaking of death and judgment, as if they had never heard of such things before. And they were not helped by two surly, ill-mannered clergymen, who seemed to be just as wise as themselves.'

Wesley preached a powerful sermon, resulting in John Darley's conversion; it is reported that Darley returned to Dunstable a changed man. It was Darley who in 1797, with others, applied to the Lord Bishop of Lincoln for a licence to register the house of Thomas Summerfield as a place of worship. In 1812 Darley opened his own workshop in Church Street, inviting people in to sing, pray and read the Bible.

The first chapel, built in 1831, was burned down in 1844 as the result of an incendiary attack on adjoining farm buildings. It was rebuilt in 1845. By 1853 the church supported a Wesleyan day school that had 100 pupils and also had a library. Disaster struck again in September 1908 when the second chapel was also burned down. How this fire started remains unknown, but that summer there had been incendiary outbreaks in the area.

Undeterred, the Methodists pushed on with even more ambitious plans for a new church on a grand scale, with a spire that would be seen for miles around. The present building opened in December 1909 with an overflowing congregation and Revd Dr John Scott Lidgett preaching. The architect was G. E. Withers of Withers and Meredith.

A fine organ was installed in 1910, which is still in use today. The church offered support during both world wars by opening a canteen to feed men and women who were serving in the forces. Throughout the remainder of the twentieth century and into the twenty-first century the Square Methodist Church continued to evolve as a place of Christian witness and worship in the town. The church

The Methodist Church overlooking a revamped square today.

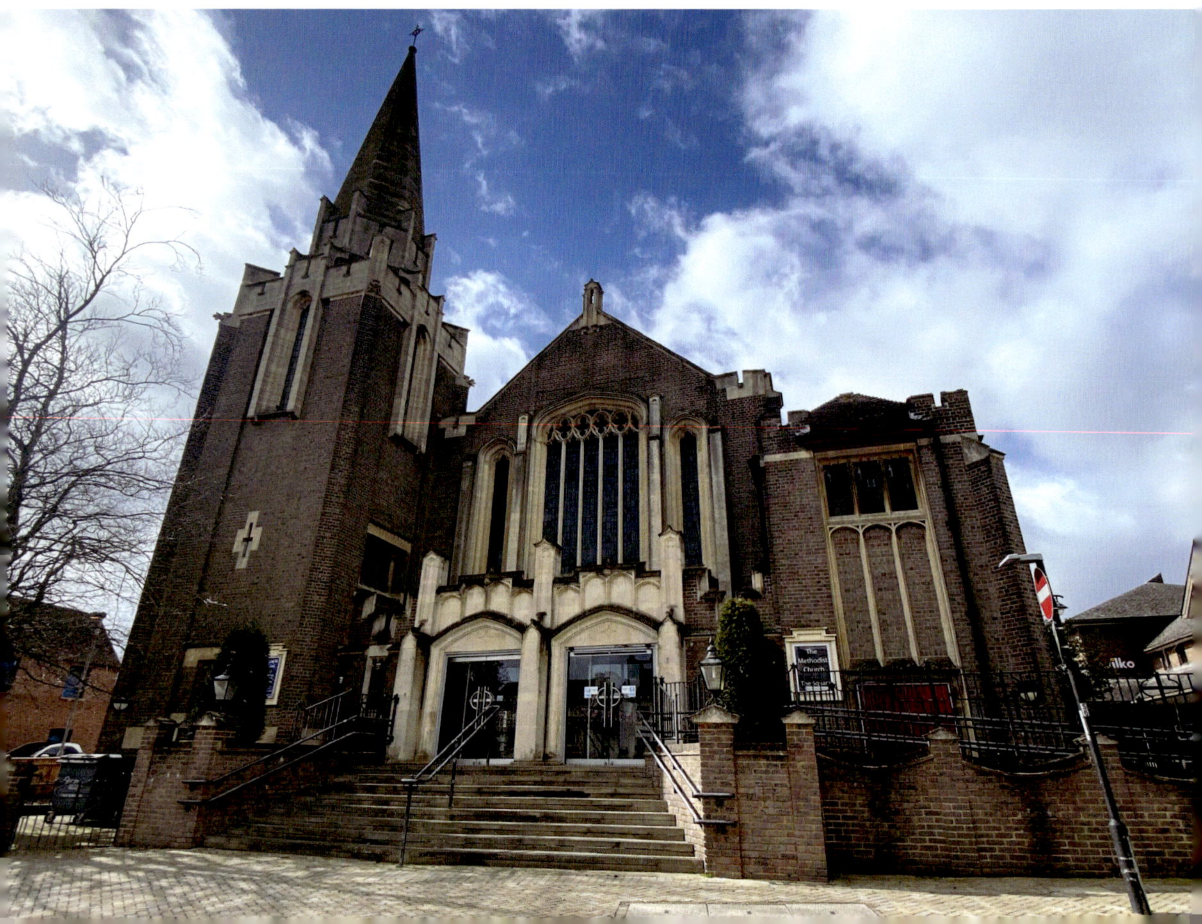

completed a building project in September 2009 which opened up the front of the church and improved access and the welcome area.

One of the more recent historical findings is the previous work of the Manse Committee and the Church Working Guild. In 1956, the then minister's wife, Mrs Brook, gathered together eighteen ladies with a view to forming a Manse Committee. There followed coffee mornings, strawberry evenings, car rallies, Caledonian Markets, Harvest Suppers and Gather Rounds. In 1959 they started holding a Cup Final Coffee Morning on the first Saturday in May, though that was before the M1 bypassed Dunstable and all the traffic came by the front door of the church – a sight to behold.

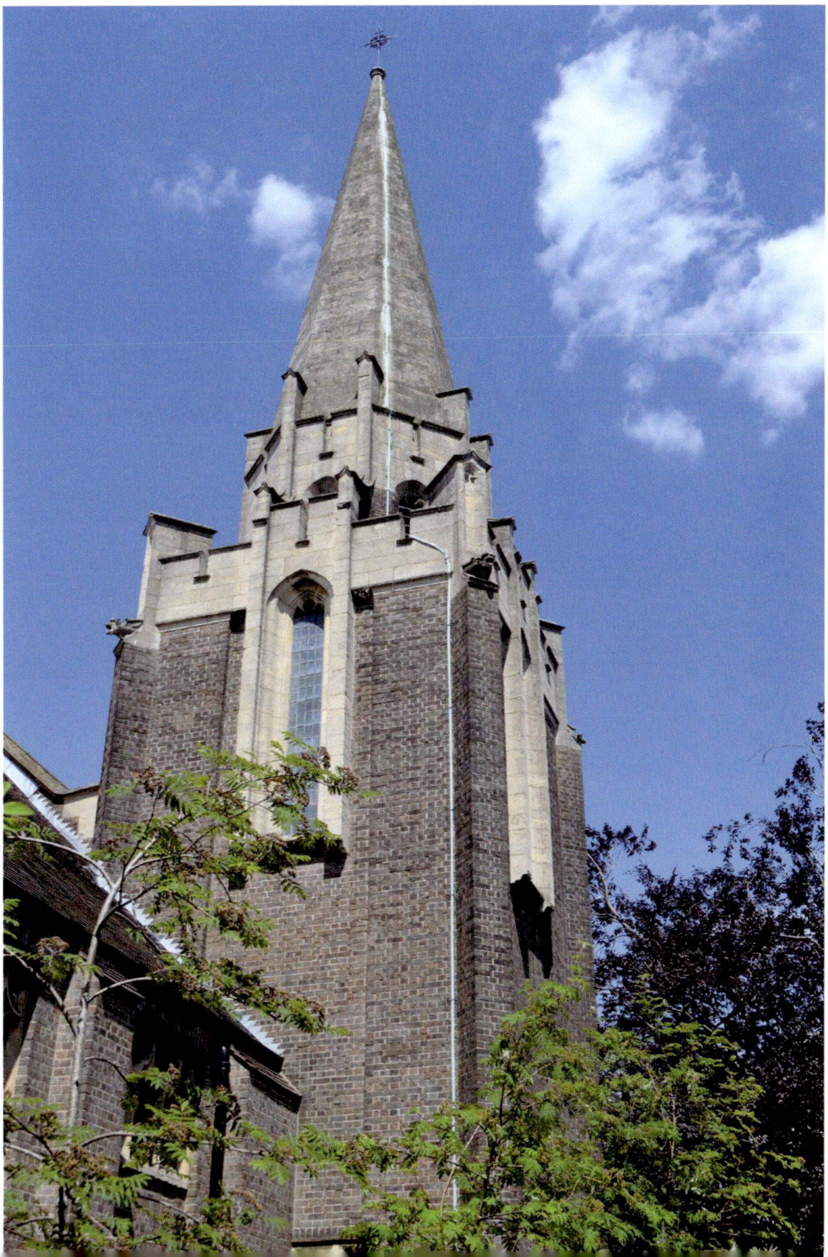

The spire of the Methodist Church, the building designed by architect G.E. Withers.

39. Lloyds Bank, High Street North

The eastern side of High Street North used to be dominated by banks – NatWest, Lloyds and Barclays. Only two remain at the time of writing, with NatWest the latest to announce its closure in 2023. The latter had been here since 1964 on the corner of High Street North and Church Street. An earlier bank had stood on this site, with the Westminster Bank taking over the small Barnard's Bank at the beginning of the twentieth century.

Further along the street is Lloyds Bank, which was built in 1923 on the site of a former ironmonger's shop that had been bought by the bank in 1920 from Wood and Co. The original shop was occupied by J. Chambers and Son, who were tenants of the trustees of the charity of Jane Cart. It was a large enterprise that occupied a substantial site with many outbuildings and had been in existence since 1763.

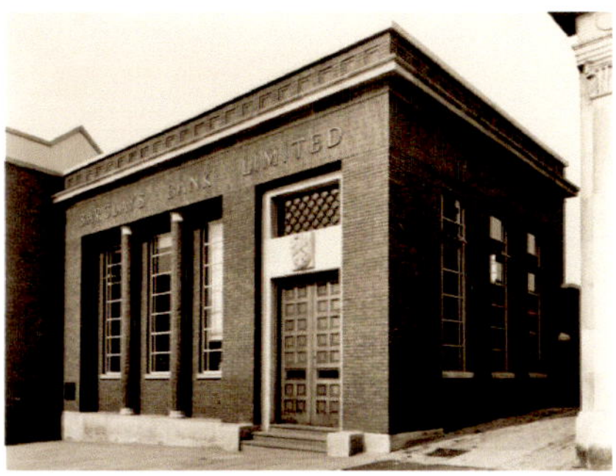

Left: The Parrott and Dunham-designed bank in Dunstable, long since demolished.

Below: Lloyds Bank, which opened in 1923.

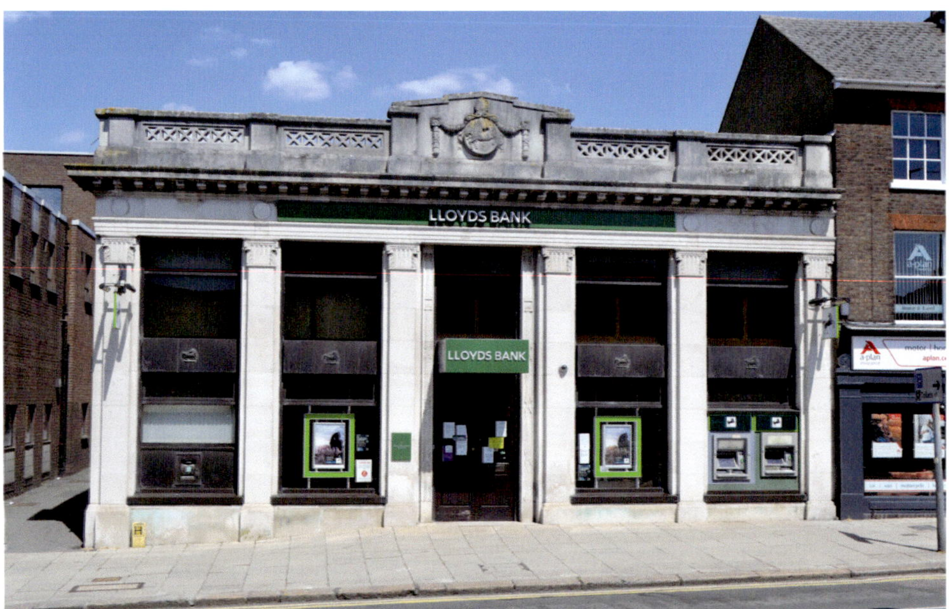

Next door to Lloyds was Barclays bank, its more modern building built on the site of Dunstable's first main post office. The post office moved in 1912 to what was then a new building in High Street North, later known as the 'Old Post Office' and eventually became the Department of Health and Social Security Office.

Barclays has a strong history in the area as they took over the small local family bank Bassett's. Bassett's started in the early nineteenth century and were initially established in 1812 in nearby Leighton Buzzard when a Quaker draper called Peter Bassett opened a bank in the town. It was passed to his son John Dollin Bassett in 1823, who took over the £9,000 capital and a partner brought in a further £3,000. A branch eventually opened in 1823 and was a local competitor to the nearby Barnard's Bank. In 1826 a rumour circulated that the banks were short of money, with people rushing to their banks demanding the gold that was 'promised on demand' on the bank notes. The smaller banks collapsed and only Bassett's survived locally.

The previous bank on the site of Barclays was designed by architects Parrott and Dunham, pictured in the 1930s, a significantly more inviting building than the current modern structure.

4c. The Former Post Office, DHSS Offices and Telephone Exchange

On High Street North is the Gothic-style old post office building, DHSS offices and former telephone exchange. It was built on the site of Manor House, which in 1885 was occupied by Dr George W. Murphy who was Medical Officer of Health to Dunstable Urban District and Medical Officer and Public Vaccinator to Dunstable District, Luton Union. At the end of the nineteenth century the Manor House was used as a girl's boarding and day school, called the Manor House School. At the beginning of the twentieth century it was converted back into residential use.

By 1912 a new building was present and was known as the 'New Post Office' because it replaced the earlier post office, opposite the old town hall, where Barclays is today. It has been designed in the Gothic style with a frontage of dark red brickwork with Monk's Park stone used for most of the windows, doorways, mouldings and dressings and a larger gable filled with a chequered pattern of white stone and flints. It was eventually replaced by a more modern post office in 1963 but was still being used for sorting until 1984 when that service was transferred to Milton Keynes and the building was put up for sale. By 1986 and with the premises behind the building rebuilt, it became the centralised Dunstable DHSS offices.

As well as being a post office, the building also contained the Dunstable Telephone Exchange. This service started in 1897, in the old offices of the *Dunstable Borough Gazette* on the corner of High Street North and Albion Street. In 1912, when the GPO took over from the National Telephone Company,

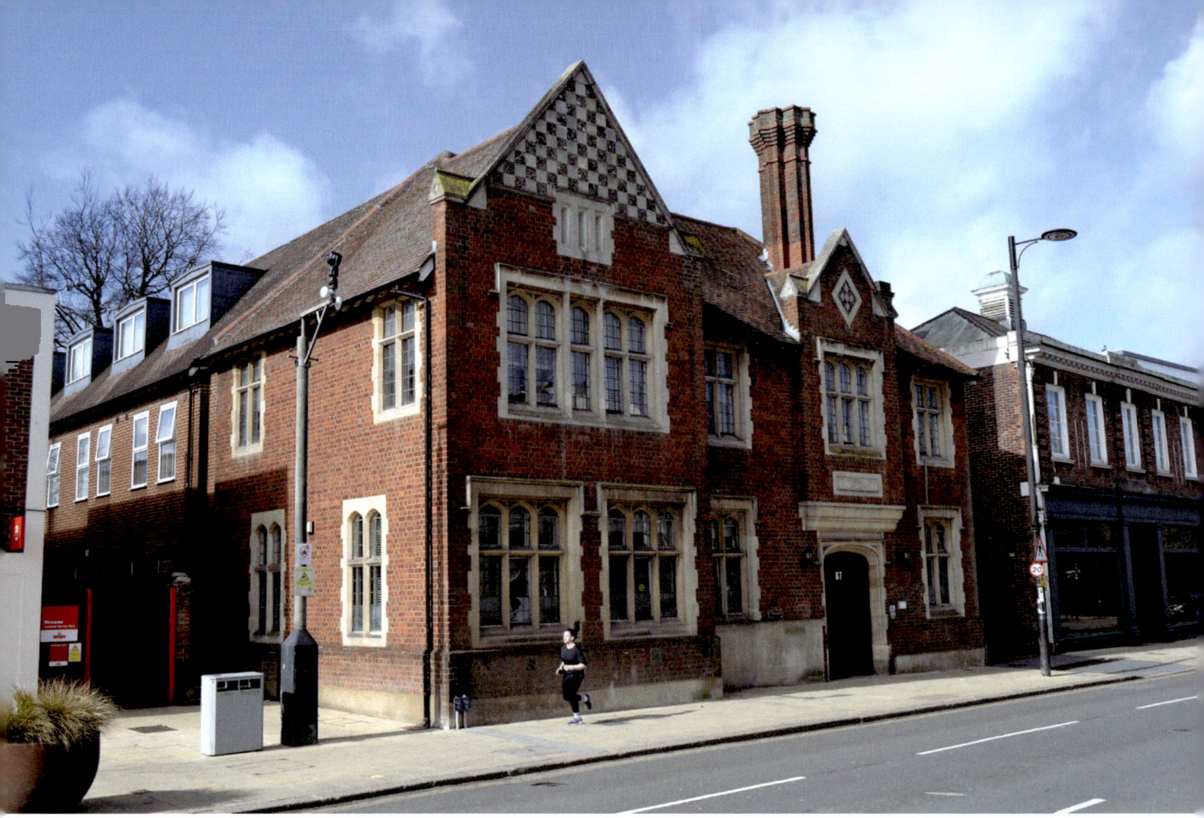

Above: A building of many uses, from post office to telephone exchange.

Below: A Gothic-style frontage on High Street North, but also the former DHSS offices for the town.

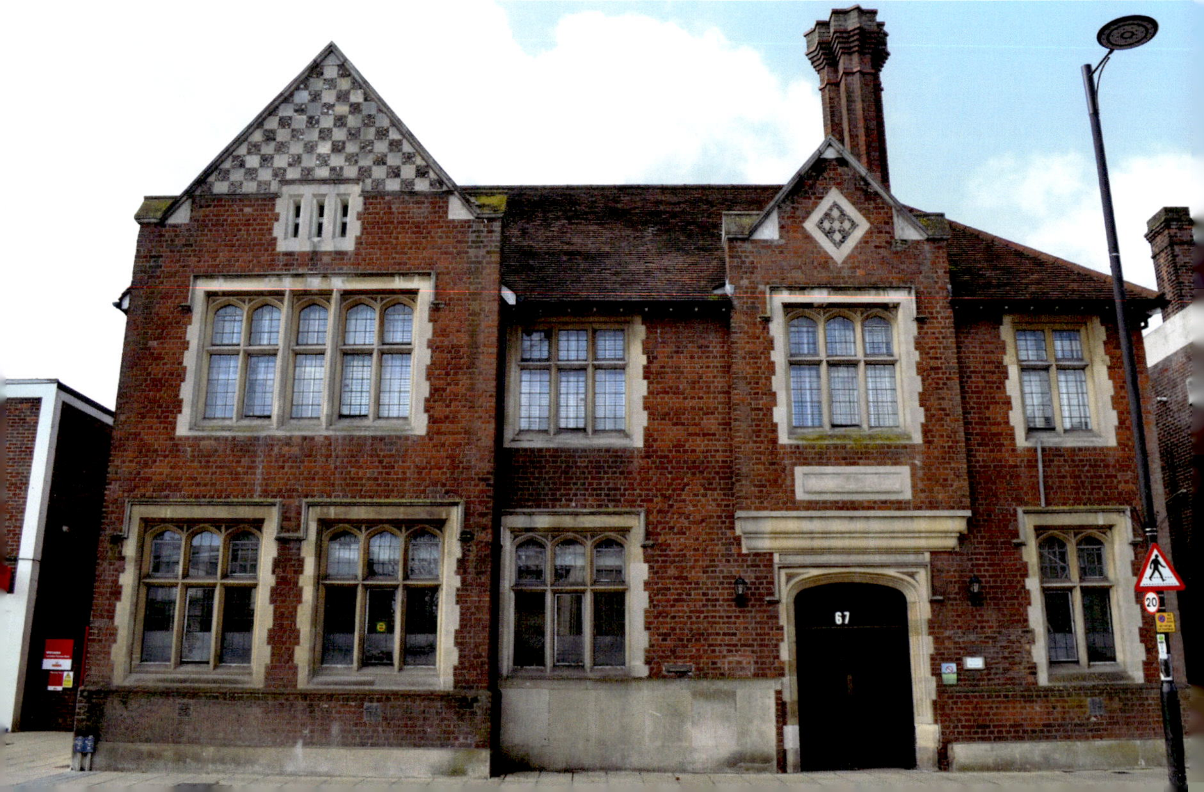

the Telephone Exchange moved into the post office building here. The uptake of telephones was initially very slow, with local people harbouring suspicions of them. By 1916, there were still only fifty-eight telephones connected to the Dunstable PO Exchange, but this increased after the Second World War. By December 1960 the Exchange became automatic and was later taken over by the Luton Telephone Exchange. Today the building is used by the NHS.

41. Petropolis House

Another fine-looking building on the corner of Friars Walk is what was originally known as Petropolis House. It was built in 1930 to replace the original police station in Icknield Street. By 1932 the headquarters of the Luton Division of the County Police had relocated here from Luton.

In March 1968 townsfolk were invited to hand in any guns to the police station. A number of firearms were still in circulation that had been obtained during the Second World War and it became illegal to possess them without a proper certificate. Those who returned guns were reassured that there would be

Once the town's police station, Petropolis House is now offices.

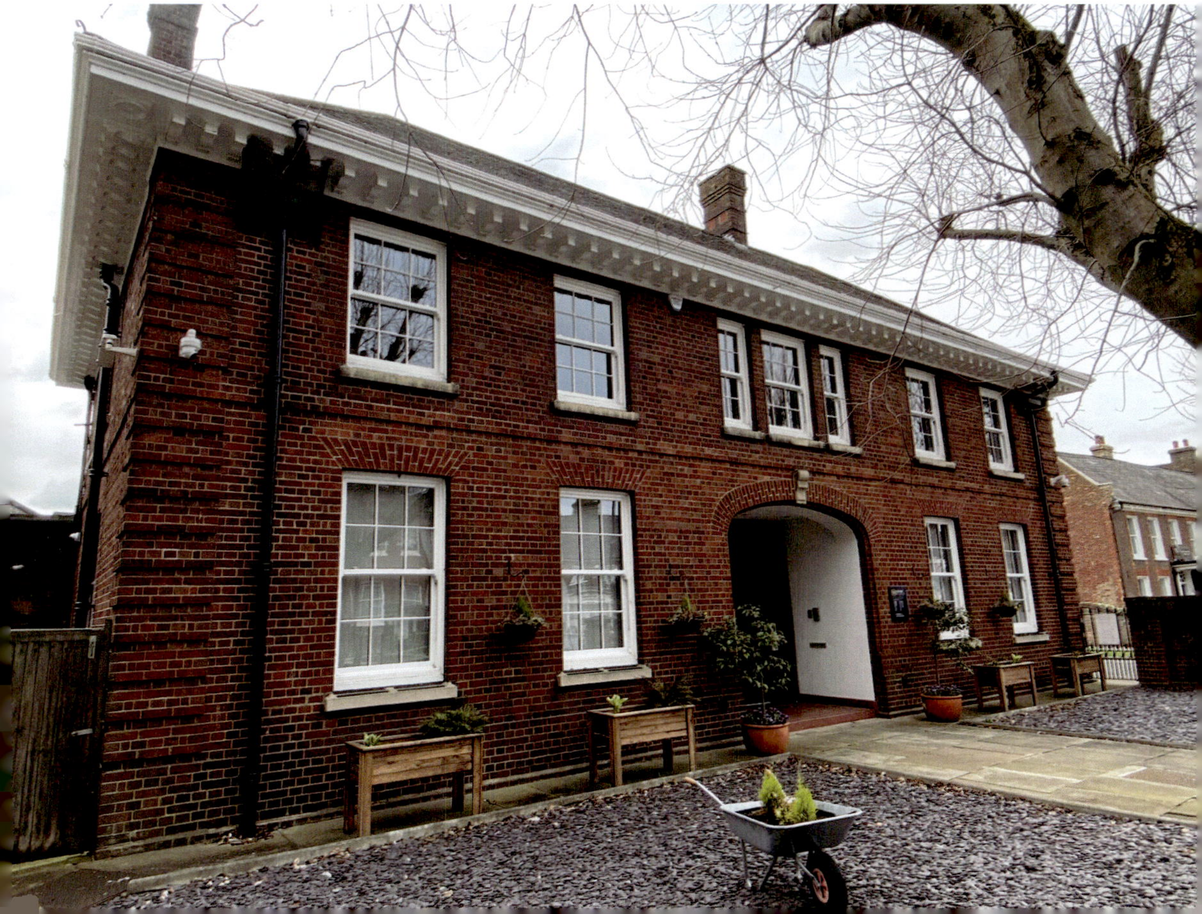

no repercussions or questions asked. One return, however, that did raise eyebrows was a semi-automatic sub-machine gun.

The current police station in West Street was built in the mid-1970s and this building was bought by a petrol company and converted into offices – hence its name becoming Petropolis House. The building today remains in use as local offices but with no links to the petroleum industry.

42. The Former Union Social Club and Cinema

On High Street North one of the more stand-out buildings is the former cinema, built between 1936 and 1937 to the designs of Leslie H. Kemp. Before it was built this was the site of Cooper's hat factory, and before that it was the site of Burr's Brewery.

This was a cinema with an interior once typical of the ambitious art deco schemes executed for Union Cinemas Ltd in the 1930s, an emulation of the still more elaborate Granada cinemas but in a distinctive idiom. This policy eventually bankrupted the company in 1937 and few, if any, other Union cinemas survive in comparable condition. Leslie Kemp was a prolific cinema designer of the period, but few of his buildings survive. The Regal Camberwell (LB Southwark) is a simpler design which is already listed.

Union Cinemas Ltd was taken over in the year that it opened in 1937 by Associated British Cinemas. The name was changed to The ABC, although the Union sign remained on the front of the building until April 1960. The cinema

The Union in 1953 – this can be dated as it is showing the film *Our Girl Friday*, which was out that year.

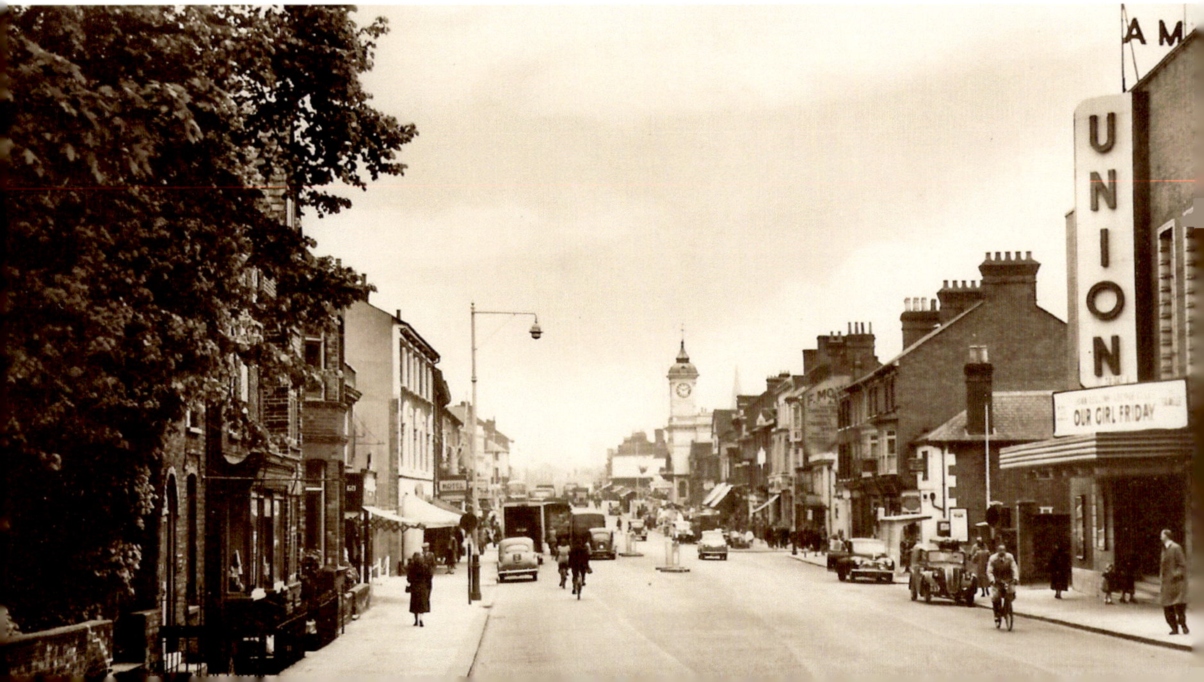

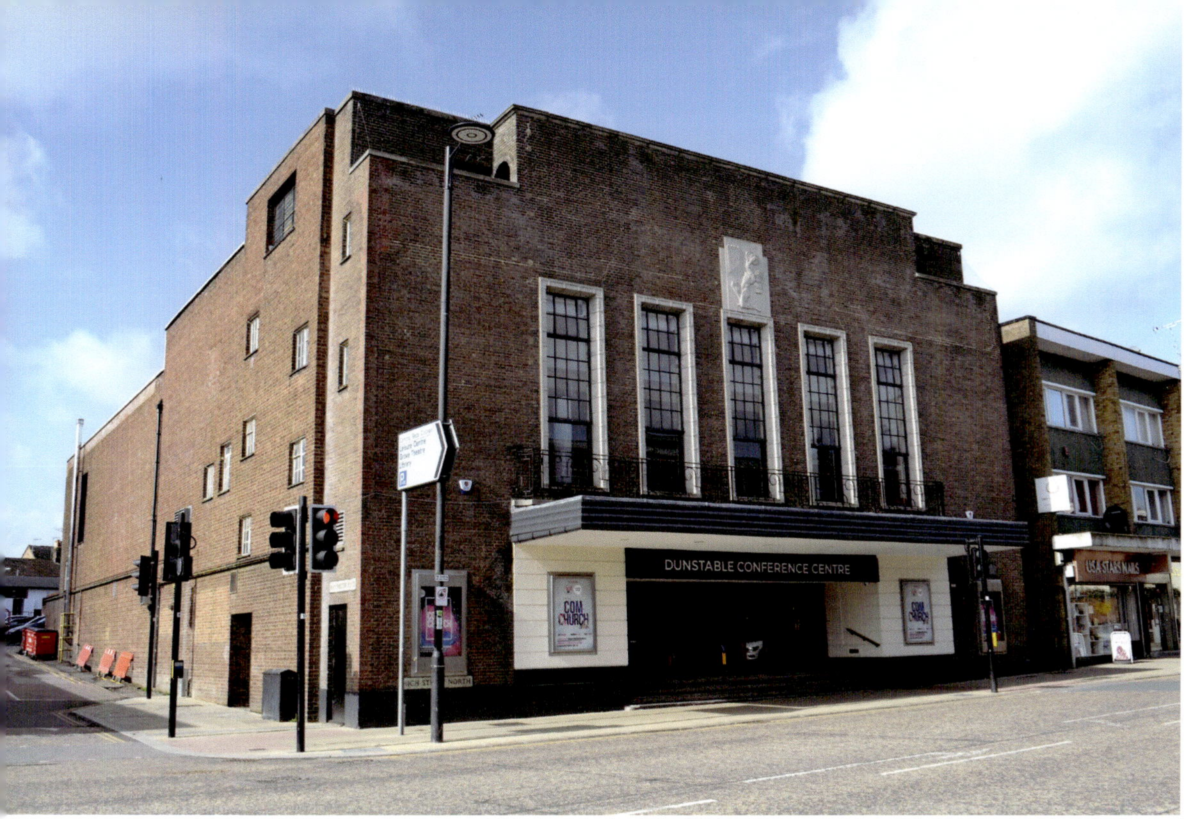

Above: The art deco building today.

Below: One of the few remaining former cinema buildings by architect Leslie H. Kemp.

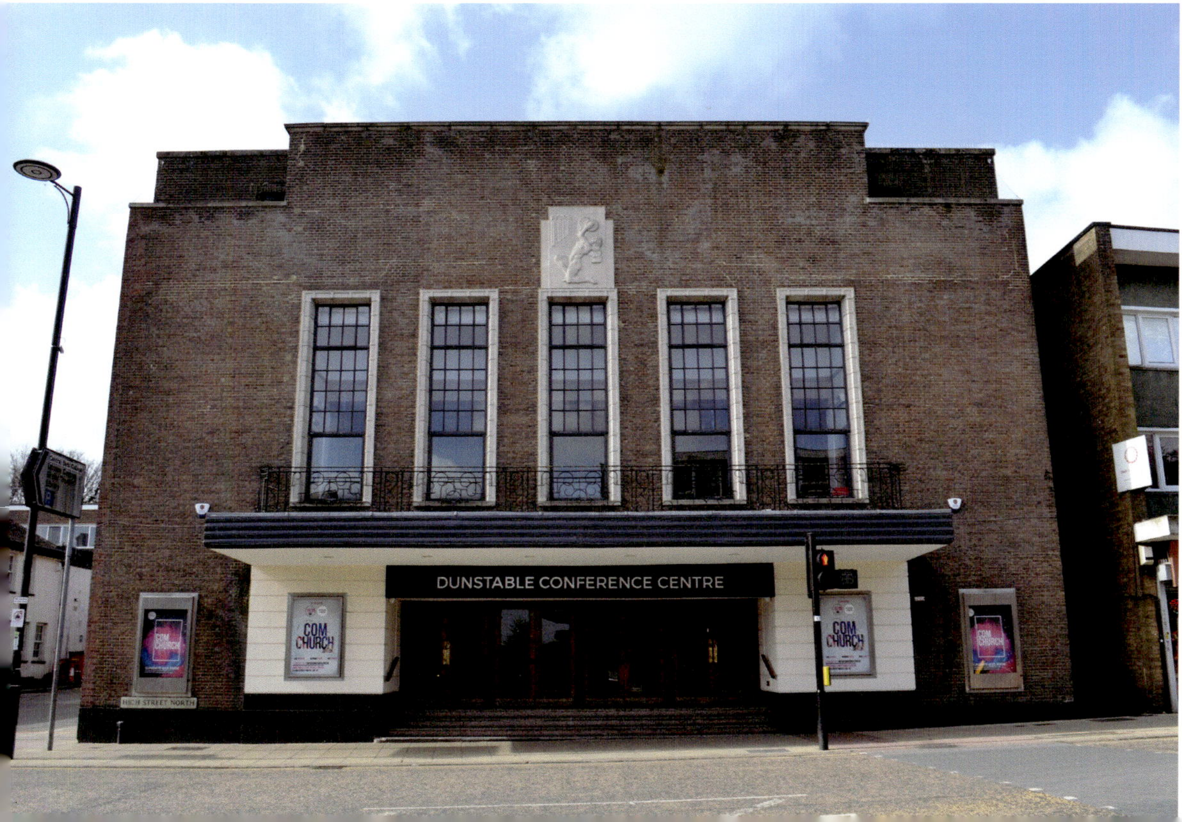

seated 1,048 patrons in the stalls and 384 in the circle, with an orchestra pit in front of the screen. One of its busiest years was 1953 when many children watched Queen Elizabeth II's coronation. The cinema remained popular during the 1950s and 1960s including with the Pakistani Film Society, who held their meetings here until 1963 when they went to the Ritz in Luton. The effect of television impacted on custom, and by the late 1960s numbers dwindled. The Union closed as a cinema in 1973, despite attempts to integrate bingo from 1969. The building became solely used for bingo from 1973 and ultimately became a nightclub. It has survived little altered and by 2011 was reopened as a popular conference centre.

43. Old Fire Station, High Street North

This is a building that could almost be missed as it is dominated by the former Ashton Grammar School and municipal buildings on either side of it. Yet it is a building of importance to the town's heritage. Between 1939 and 1965 this was the town's fire station. It is built with local Kensworth grey bricks and has a keystone above with the borough arms and the door opening margin, front cornice, piers and wall copings all made from Clipsham stone. It housed two fire engines which had previously been kept at the old town hall. Designed by architect W. F. Wilkins and built by contractors Robinson and White, it was formally opened on 28 January 1939 by Lord Luke of Pavenham KBE along with public conveniences to the rear of the building.

The town's former fire station.

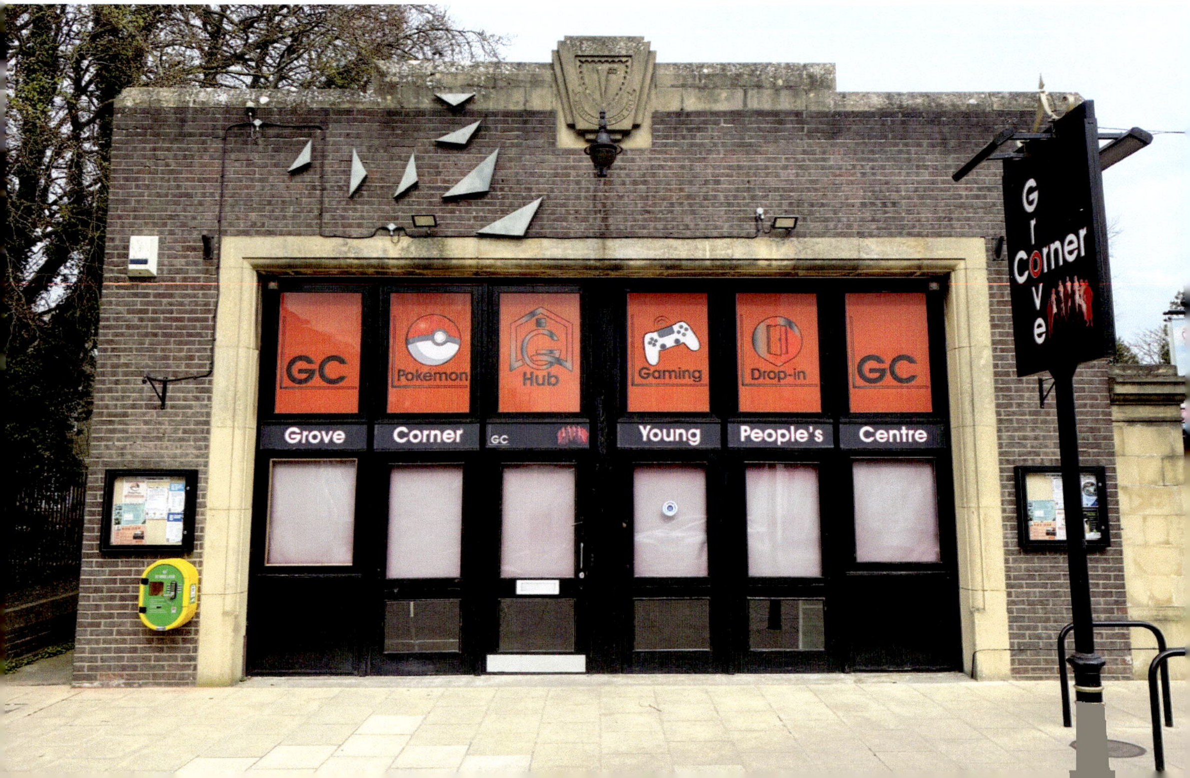

By the 1960s a larger station was required for more modern appliances, so a new station was built on the corner of High Street North and Brewers Hill at a cost of over £100,000. This was opened in October 1965 by Lord Stonham, Under Secretary for the Home Office, and the Mayor and Mayoress of Dunstable.

The building became used by the St John's Ambulance Brigade and today is a centre for young people.

44. The Former Chiltern Road School

Another building that has a hidden history in the side streets of Dunstable is the former Chiltern Road School, which shut in 1974 and was then occupied by a Teachers' Centre for a while. By 1982 the school was converted into studios for Chiltern Radio. It is the building's latter use that ensures its inclusion here.

Chiltern Radio was a highly successful independent radio station which was part of the Independent Broadcasting Authority's expansion programme of commercial radio stations across the country in the 1980s. The franchise was to be a 'twin station' centred on Luton and Bedford and covering significant parts of Hertfordshire, Bedfordshire and Buckinghamshire. This coverage area included the Luton-Dunstable conurbation, containing the largest population centre in the East of England region. It was the countryside surrounding the Chiltern Hills that inspired the name Chiltern Radio.

The programmers at Chiltern Radio captured the spirit of a sophisticated population in harmony with its surrounding countryside and incorporated it into the sound of the station. The music of the radio station was as lively and fashionable as the proximity to London would ever demand, yet its presentation shouted the beauty and inspiration of the surrounding countryside. Chiltern's attractive location ensured that professional broadcasting talent was always in good supply.

The programme staff were altogether above the average in talent and innovation. This was just as well as Chiltern saw itself as a 'full service' radio station and designed a programme schedule that was modern, fun, lively and exciting, yet incorporated public service specialist programmes such as *Kid's Stuff*, an educational children's programme; the Italian language programme *L'Ora Italiano*; a religious magazine programme on Sunday mornings; *In Town and Village* for general interest, where the production team visited a community in the region each week; and many shorter programme features such as fishing, sport and farming. Chiltern produced specialist music programmes too with classical, jazz and country music.

Unlike other areas in the UK, the first local radio service for 'Herts, Beds and Bucks' came from the independent or commercial sector. In most other areas in the country the BBC had always managed to be first. This was an advantage for Chiltern Radio, and the programme team were determined to maintain its primacy when BBC Radio Bedfordshire eventually came to the area several years later.

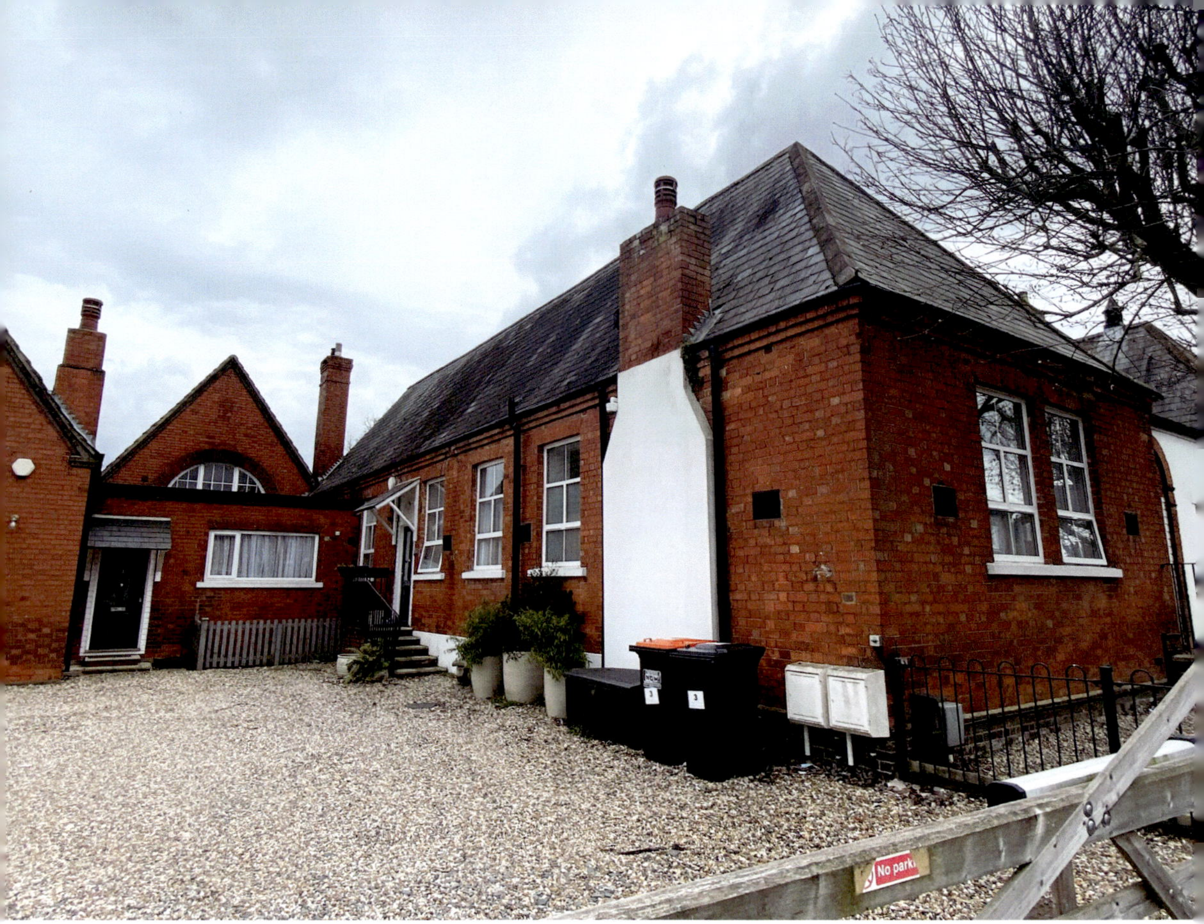

Above: Chiltern Road School, becoming the centre of the region's radio station.

Below: Perhaps a reminder of the building's initial intended use.

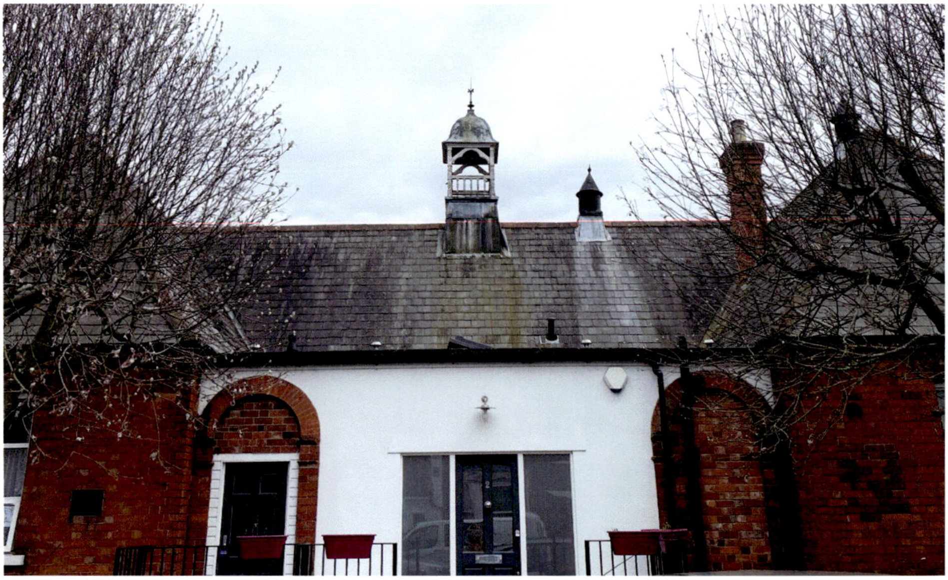

On 1 June 1982, Chiltern expanded into Bedford with studios on Goldington Road. This was joined on 30 November 1986 with Northants Radio from Northampton, and on 15 October 1989 with Horizon Radio from Milton Keynes. The Hot FM network transmitted on the FM services of 97.6 Chiltern FM, 96.9 Chiltern FM, Northants 96, Horizon Radio, followed later by Oasis Radio, Severn Sound and Galaxy Radio. For a while Galaxy Radio and Horizon Radio operated a slightly more edgy 'Hotter Mix' format, although switched back again to the 'Hot FM' for networked programming. Supergold transmitted on the AM services of Chiltern Radio and Northants Radio, followed later by Severn Sound and Invicta Radio. Stations would broadcast from their own studios until 7 p.m., then share programmes from Dunstable overnight.

In 1994, the GWR Group acquired the network and began rebranding the stations in September 1995 – the FM stations as part of their Mix Network and Gold stations as Classic Gold Digital Network. Shared programming moved to Bristol. In May 2005, the GWR Group merged with Capital Radio to form Gcap Media, which was further bought out by Global Radio in 2008, and eventually became the Heart Radio network.

Today the building is residential and may perhaps still echo to the sound of children playing or the jingles of yesterday's Chiltern Radio.

45. St Mary's Roman Catholic Church, West Street

This is a wonderful building and reflects the many architectural styles found in Dunstable. St Mary's Roman Catholic Church on West Street is an ambitious and bold design of the early 1960s, built from designs by architects Desmond Williams & Associates of Manchester at a cost of £72,000. The builders were R. Willis & Son. Work started late in 1961 and the completed building was opened and blessed by Bishop Parker on 15 March 1964. The church was built to accommodate a maximum of 800 people, including provision for about 120 in the large gallery.

In 1927 the establishment of a parish in Dunstable was entrusted by the Bishop to the Spanish Congregation of St Vincent de Paul, based at Potters Bar. Before that, local Catholics had to travel to Luton or Leighton Buzzard to attend Mass. In 1935 a small red-brick Gothic church dedicated to the Immaculate Conception was built. This church survives as part of the present parish hall.

According to the brief accounts in the *Catholic Building Review* of 1965 and 1964, the circular form of the design was driven by the L-shaped site, in which the church sits at the intersection, and by the desire to ensure that the congregation was as near as possible to the sanctuary. The planning of the church did not envisage a central altar, but an altar and sanctuary at one end of the axis, allowing for westward celebration.

Alongside the new church a contemporary presbytery and offices were constructed, and a later hut was built to the north of the church adjacent to a

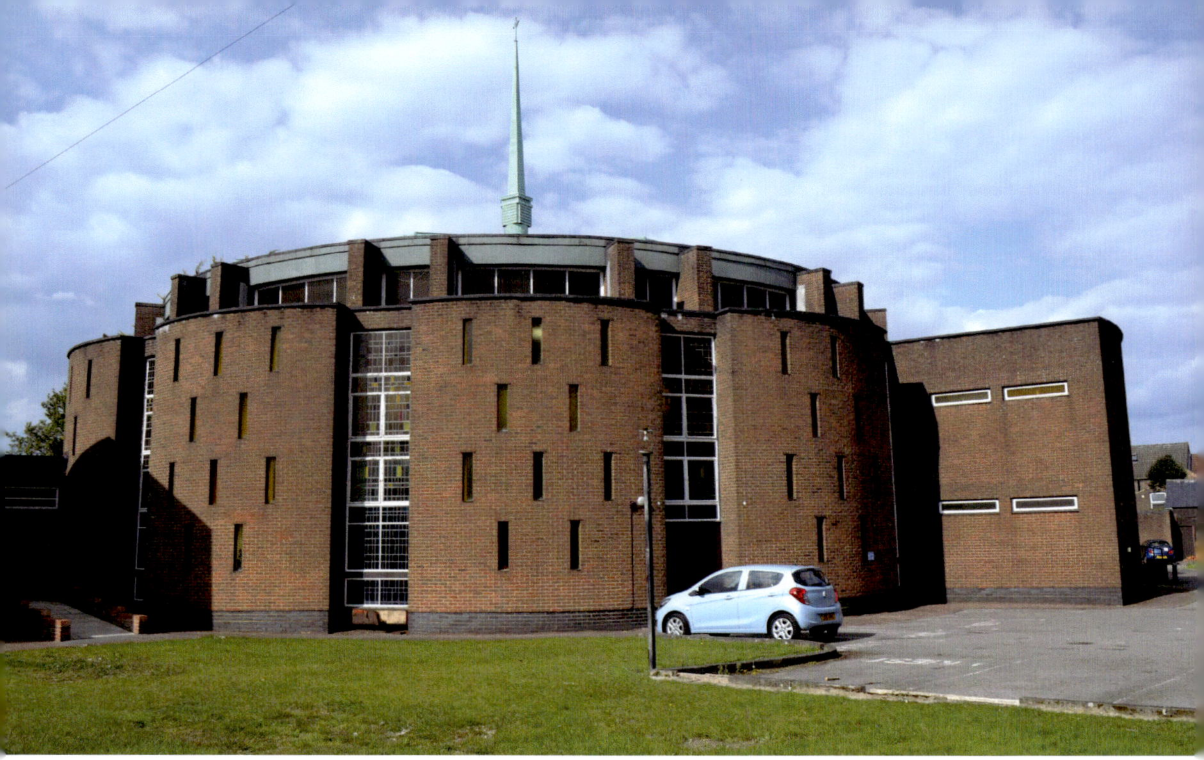

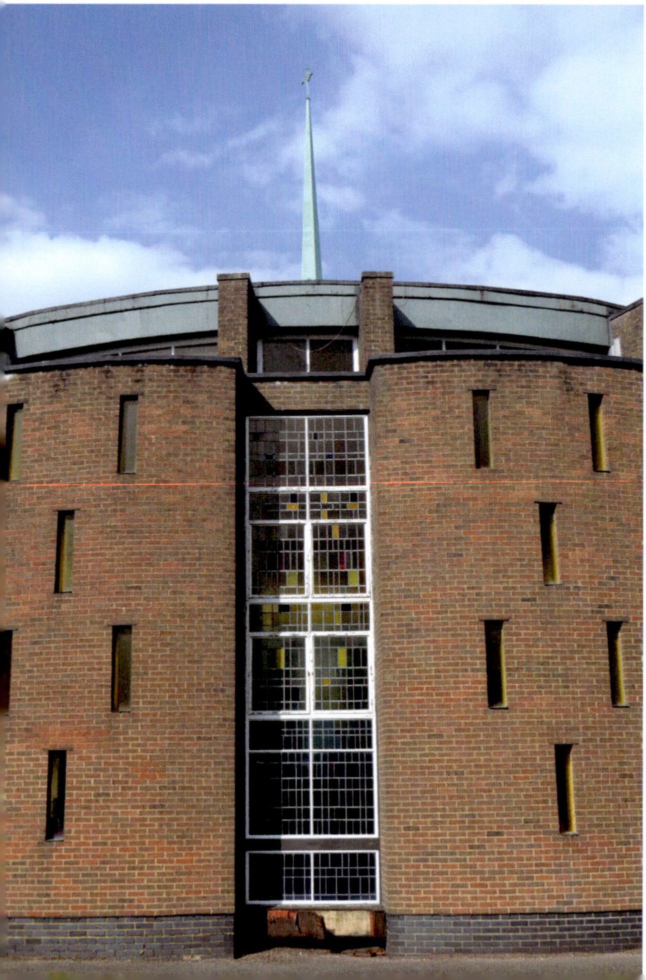

Above: St Mary's Roman Catholic Church.

Left: Opened in 1964, the building remains little altered and is a testament to its architects, Desmond Williams and Associates.

(2000) Garden of Remembrance. The church has not been heavily altered since its completion, though the baptistery has been repurposed as a shop. Desmond Williams & Associates designed a number of modern churches, including the Roman Catholic Church of St Augustine, Manchester, 1966–68 with a notable reredos by Robert Brumby (Grade II); the Roman Catholic Church of St Dunstan, Birmingham, 1966–68 (Grade II); and the Roman Catholic Church of St Michael, Penn, Wolverhampton, 1967–68 (Grade II). Desmond Williams worked with Arthur Facebrother before setting up his own practice in Manchester, which in around 1970 amalgamated with W. & J. B. Ellis to become Ellis Williams Architects. Williams' work was recognised with the award of an OBE in 1988.

46. Quadrant Shopping Centre and Middle Row

In the centre of the town are two very contrasting areas that have focused primarily on retail and shopping – the ancient Middle Row and the more modern Quadrant Shopping Centre. Middle Row was originally part of the marketplace in Dunstable, but by the end of the twelfth century there was a collection of workshops and market stalls located here. By the thirteenth century some of these workshops were made more permanent by constructing them in wooden lath and plaster. It is likely that there were goldsmiths and blacksmiths located here, along with those trading from portable barrows. Some historic records also suggest that the town's prison once was located on Middle Row but was pulled down and rebuilt in 1295.

The fourteenth and fifteenth centuries saw the market grow and this area became a collective of shops, houses and enclosed paddocks known as Middle Rents. It consisted primarily of timber-framed buildings, built back-to-back and two to three storeys high.

The seventeenth and eighteenth centuries saw further change as Middle Rents catered for visitors to the market and travellers through Dunstable. This included at least five public houses, including the Rose and Crown, and up to six butchers. The publicans often had other trades in addition to their prime pub work, such as The Shoulder of Mutton and Thomas Botterill, who was a boot and shoemaker, and Mary Higgs at the Swan with Two Necks, who was a bricklayer.

Some shops survived on the High Street side through the twentieth century and up to today, with many modifications and new businesses established; however, those facing Ashton Square have struggled. Over recent years, shops have improved on the rear side, making this an attractive space generally. The cost of living crisis and COVID-19 between 2019 and 2023 have seen more properties being vacated.

In contrast is the Quadrant on the north side of High Street North, a pedestrian-only shopping area designed by Willoughby Fletcher & Associates, which was opened on 3 June 1966 by local celebrity Bob Monkhouse. At the centre of the

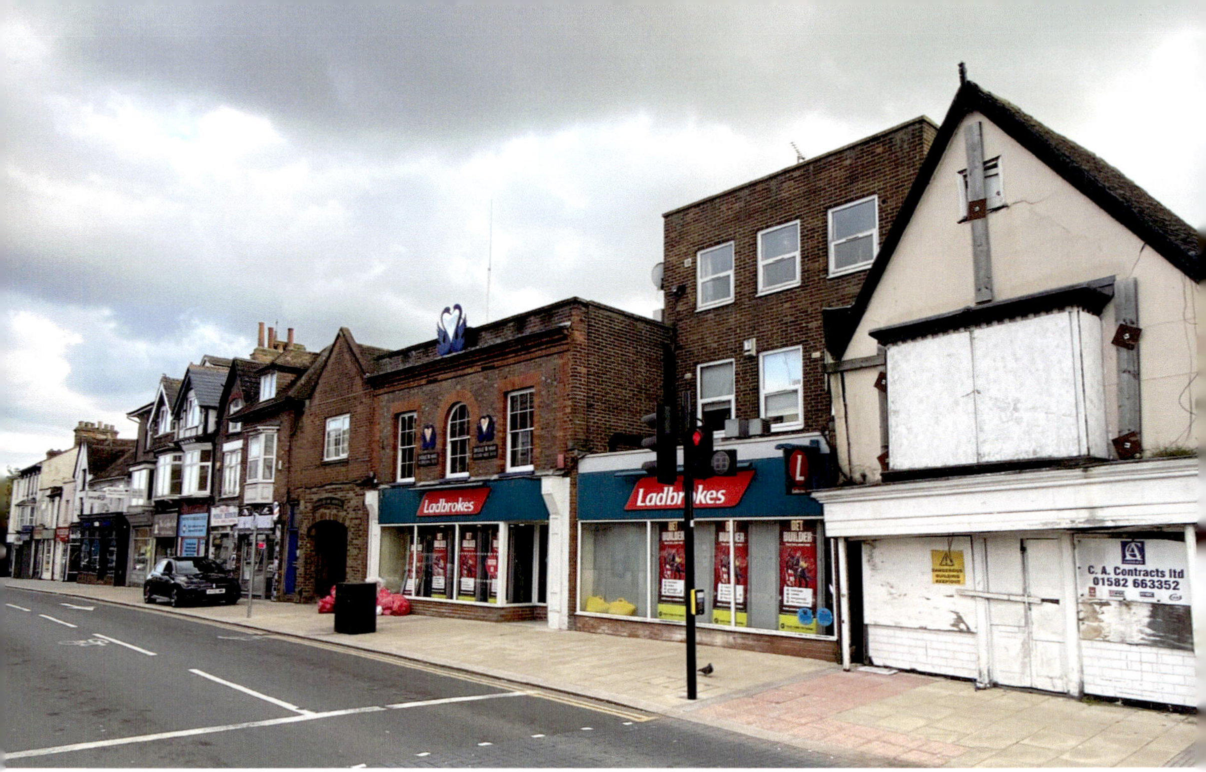

Above: Middle Row shops.

Below: The rear area of Middle Row.

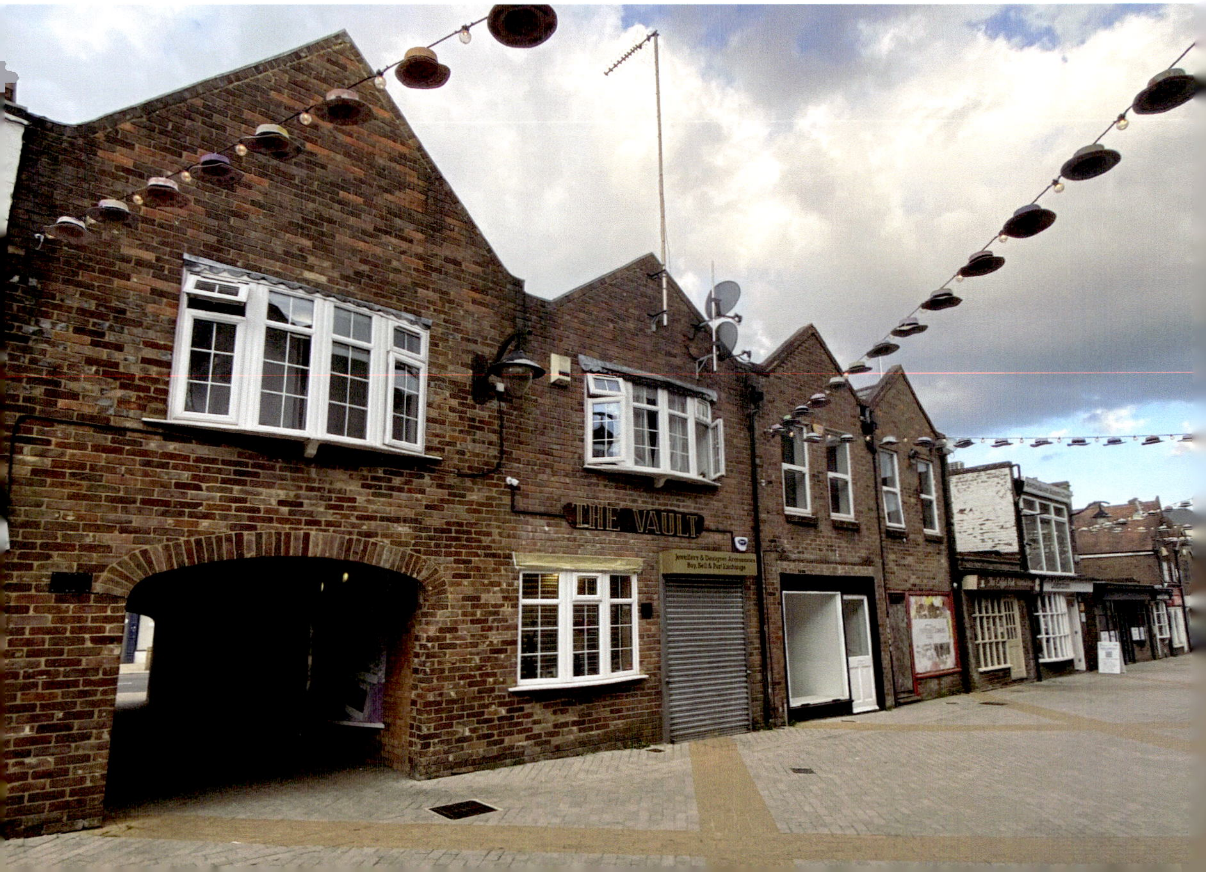

Right: The Quadrant Shopping Centre and its 'not so reliable clock' removed in 1987. (© *Dunstable Gazette*)

Below: The mural above Boots the Chemist, by William Mitchell Associates.

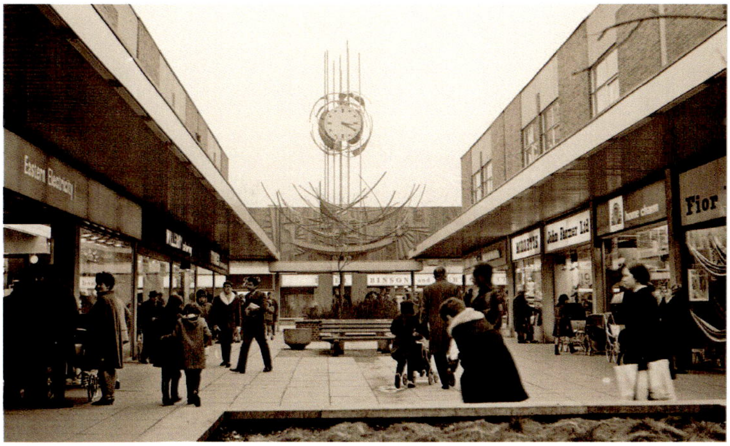

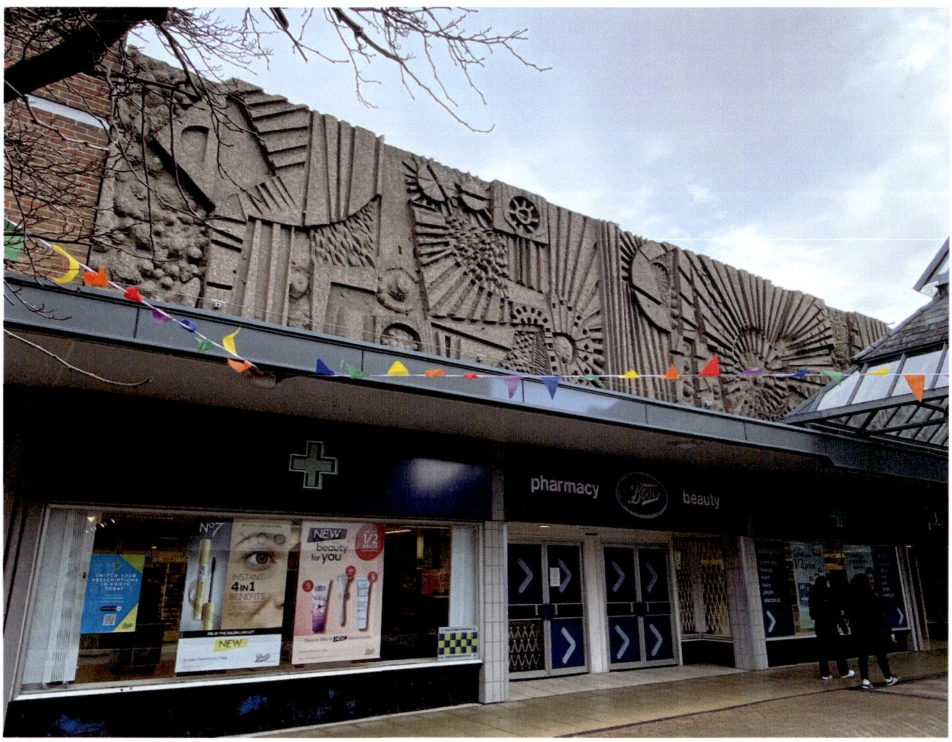

T-shaped precinct used to be the three-faced Quadrant Clock, designed by Robin Cameron Don of Scotland, which was suspended in the air by a network of curved tubular steel and translucent coloured fibre-glass panels. It rarely worked and was much despised by local residents.

The mural above Boots, however, is more reliable and certainly pleasing to the eye. It was designed by William Mitchell & Associates. I wonder how many notice it these days.

47. Frances Ashton Almshouses

These new almshouses were built to replace those demolished in West Street and are known as Frances Ashton House today. The original almshouses were built in 1715 and they were maintained by a group of trustees, as determined by Frances Ashton's will after her death in 1727. When the West Street land was sold to a property developer, the money was used to build the present Ashton Almshouses. The new buildings were officially opened on 30 December 1969 with a short service of dedication performed by the Bishop of Bedford, when the mayor of Dunstable presented each tenant with a key to their new home, complete with central heating.

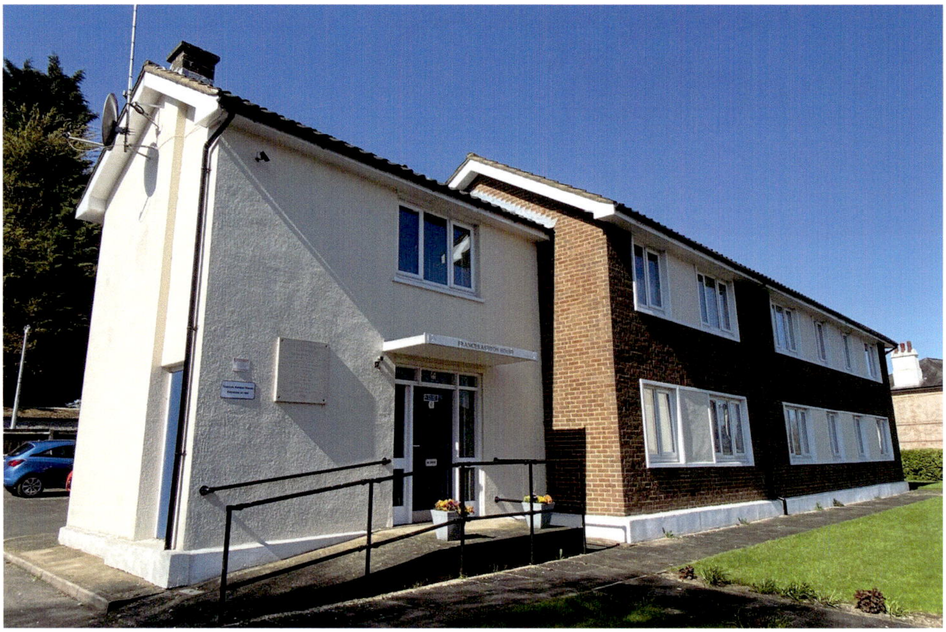

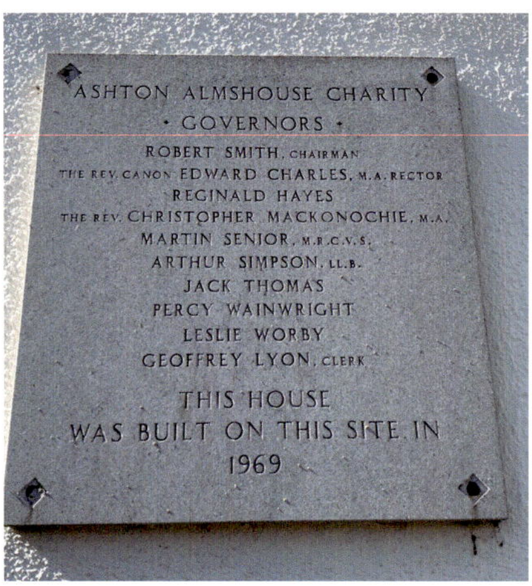

Above: A very ordinary building, but its legacy is an important part of the history of the town.

Left: Francis Ashton's legacy still lives on.

48. Salvation Army Dunstable Corps

The Salvation Army began on the streets of East London in 1865 when Methodists William and Catherine Booth abandoned the traditional concept of a church pulpit to take God's word directly to the people. The Booths preached and lived out a doctrine of practical Christianity – soup, soap and salvation – to encourage both social and spiritual transformation among society's most vulnerable and marginalised people. Their work included setting up shelters for people who were homeless, a family tracing service, running soup kitchens, helping people living in the slums and setting up rescue homes for women fleeing domestic abuse and prostitution. The couple also oversaw the world's first free labour exchange and campaigned to improve working conditions.

The movement grew rapidly outside of London and became known as the Christian Mission, with William Booth as its General Superintendent. In 1878 the name was changed to the Salvation Army and the organisation adopted a quasi-military structure with officers and members wearing a military-style uniform.

The Salvation Army movement spread rapidly across the British Isles and within decades was established across the globe in countries such as America, Canada, Australia, France, Switzerland, India, South Africa, Iceland and Germany.

The challenges people were facing in the late nineteenth century – homelessness, addiction, loneliness and unemployment – are much the same as today. The Salvation Army has continued its founders' work, tackling issues and working at the heart of communities to offer practical help, unconditional assistance and support to transform lives. Today, the Salvation Army is a church and charity that is active in virtually every corner of the world and serves in more than 130 countries.

A more modern hall that replaced the original building built in 1937, it's religious use in stark contrast to some of the grisly events on Bullpond Lane many decades ago.

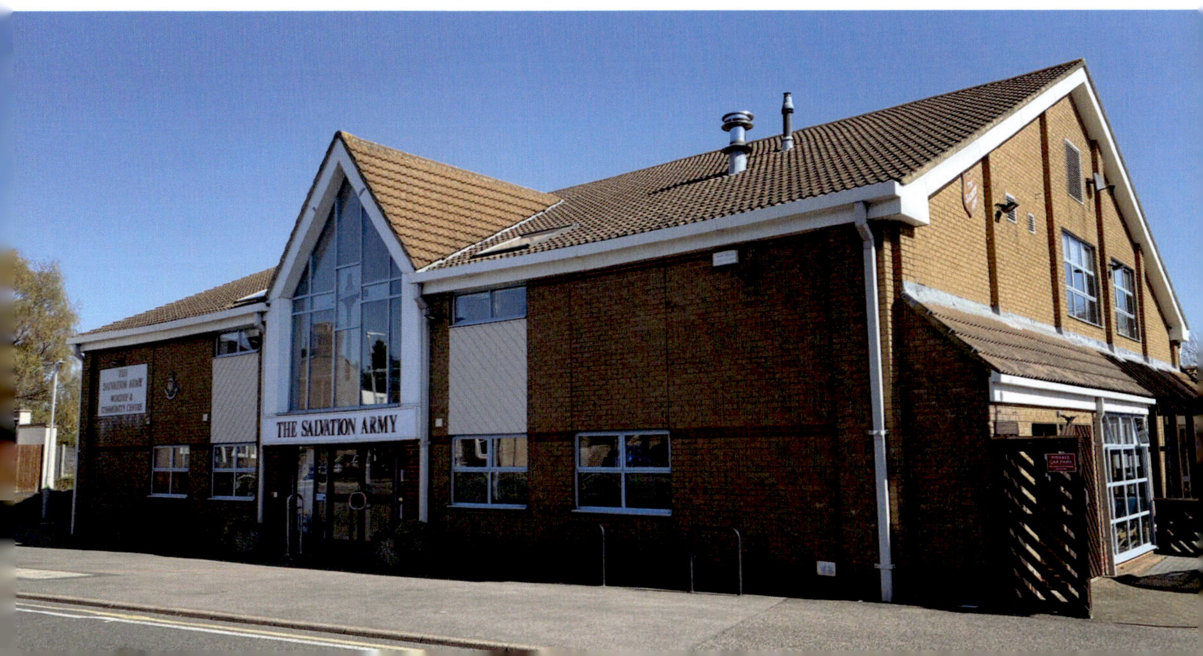

Here in Dunstable, the original hall used by the Salvation Army was built in 1937, although they have been active in the town since the beginning of the twentieth century, occupying a considerably more modern building today, which was opened on 4 June 1994. They have had close links with the Methodist Church too: Colonel Mary Booth, granddaughter of founder William Booth, visited the Methodist Church on the Square in 1944. Bullpond Lane is also one of the oldest lanes in Dunstable. The road once contained a pond and it used to lead to fields to Stipers Hill, where there was a bull ring. The cruel practice of slowly killing bulls used to be carried out there for sport and for 'better meat'.

49. The Grove Theatre/BBC Three Counties/Central Bedfordshire College

Between 2008 and 2011 Central Bedfordshire Council proposed adopting a masterplan approach to regenerating the town centre. Part of this ambitious plan was the redevelopment of the area behind and adjacent to Grove Park. This included a new theatre, BBC Three Counties venue and a revamped campus for Central Bedfordshire College, along with other retail and leisure facilities. The result is an eclectic mix of modern architecture that has provided modern facilities for the town.

Among them is the Grove Theatre, a 780-seat regional theatre that first opened its doors to the public on 21 April 2007 and was designed by Glenn Howells Architects. The first show to take place at the Grove Theatre was an opening gala that was hosted by stage and screen giant Brian Blessed on 21 April, which was followed by a week-long run of the West End hit *Joseph and the Amazing Technicolor Dreamcoat*. Following the venue's opening in April, the Grove Theatre was officially opened in July 2007 by the Duke of Gloucester and hosts many wide and varied events every year.

The new open-plan office for BBC Three Counties Radio was also a welcome addition to the area and provided the local audience greater access to the station. Many of the day-to-day needs, including broadcasting studios, production offices and the news operation, are located on the ground level, giving audiences an insight into the world of live broadcasting.

The move to Dunstable in June 2015 also coincided with the station's thirtieth birthday. Councillor Nigel Young, Executive Member for Regeneration and Dunstable Watling ward member, said at the time of the relocation to Dunstable:

> We're delighted that BBC Three Counties Radio has chosen Dunstable as their new base. Their arrival will further stimulate the regeneration of the town and is an example of the way businesses can and will benefit from the infrastructure – such as the Luton Dunstable Busway – that Central Bedfordshire Council continues to deliver. I trust the BBC share our vision of an increasing optimistic outlook for the town – one that is fast becoming a go-to destination for many

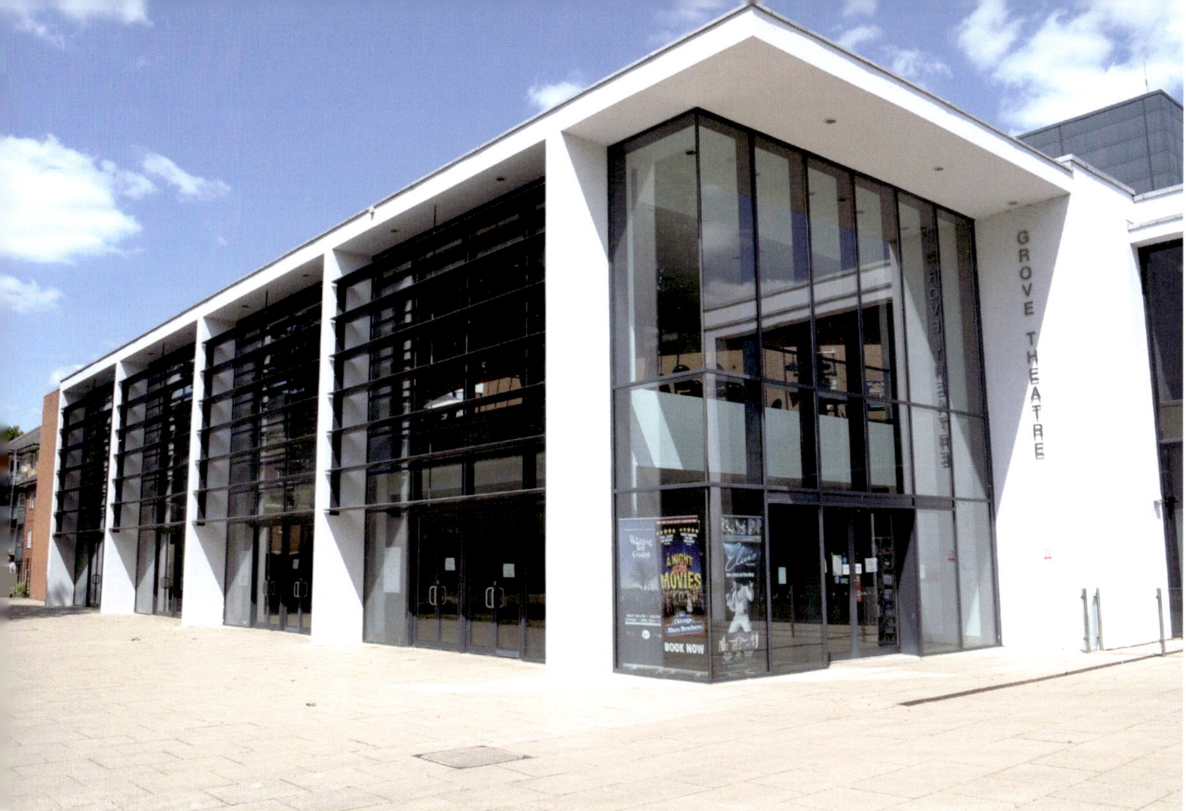

Above: The modern Grove Theatre, which opened its doors in 2007.

Below: The modern BBC offices.

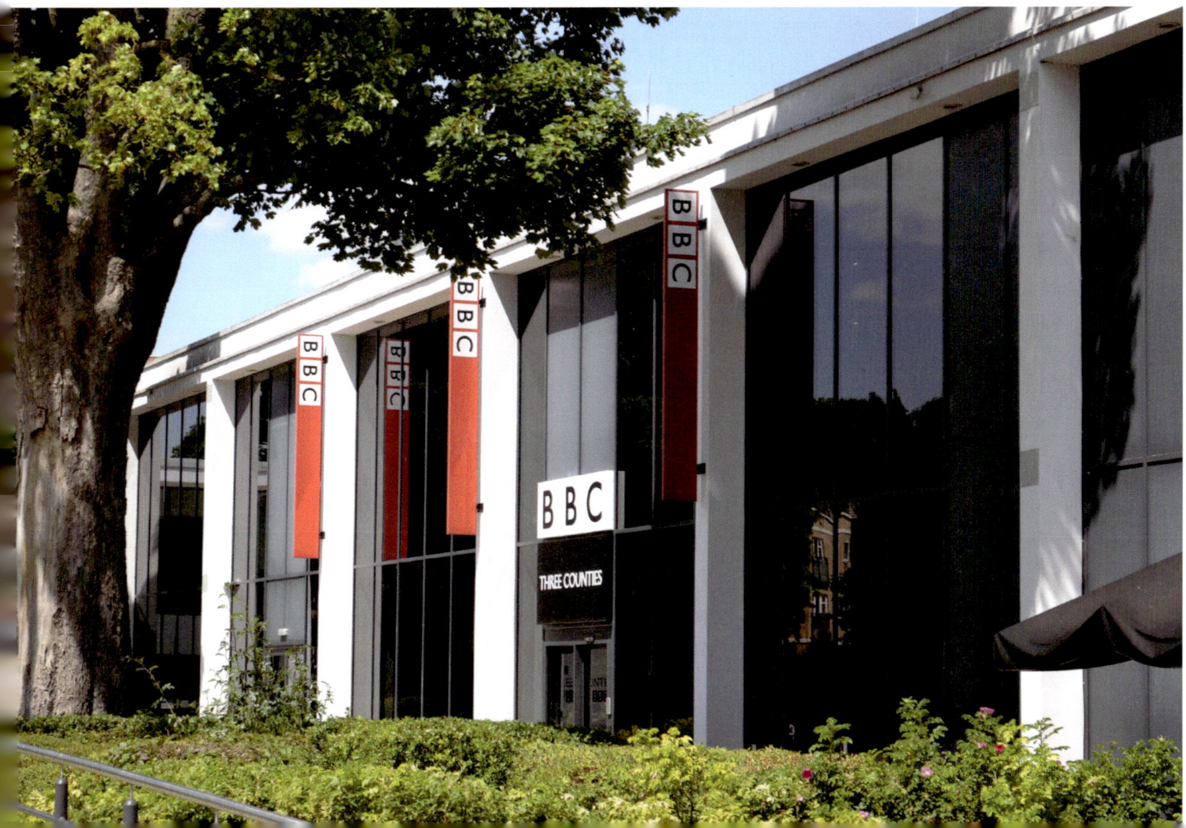

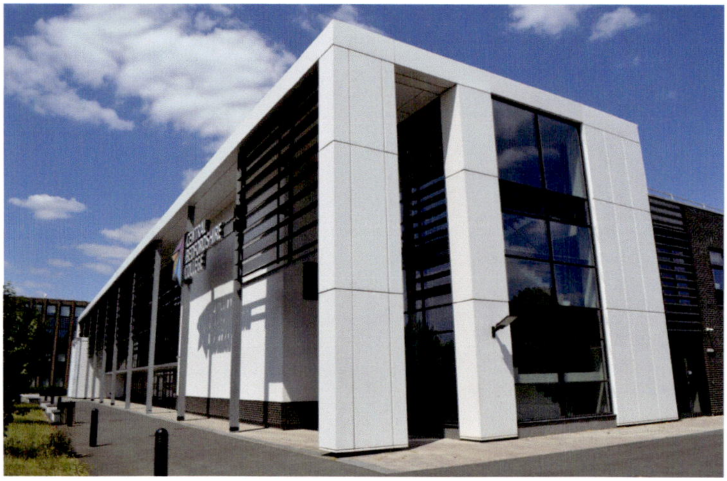

Central Bedfordshire College.

> businesses. Grove Park, in particular, is now a flourishing cultural centre for Dunstable and the welcome arrival of BBC Three Counties Radio will mean it is now fully occupied for the first time in eight years. We're thrilled to have played a part in making this transition happen for the station and wish them all the best in their new home.

In 2015, a major redevelopment of the Kingsway Campus was completed at a cost of £10 million for Central Bedfordshire College, adding to the vibrancy of this area. The architect was Atkins. Central Bedfordshire College was established in 1961 in Dunstable. On 14 January 2010, the college was renamed Central Bedfordshire College. Ali Hadawi CBE, principal and chief executive, explained that the change of name was to reflect the college's commitment to Central Bedfordshire as a whole and to be recognised as the premier post-sixteen institution in the area. Today, the college has four campuses across Central Bedfordshire: here in Dunstable and at Houghton Regis, Luton and Leighton Buzzard.

50. Incuba Centre

It seems fitting to have as the fiftieth building in this book one that is very much focussed on innovation, technology and the future – the Incuba Centre. A sod-cutting ceremony was held to mark the start of works at Central Bedfordshire College's new Incuba Innovation Centre in the town in October 2012.

The development was to include a mixture of teaching spaces and small business units built for use by those working in the renewable energy field and eventually formed part of the town's economic regeneration plan. The college's aims were 'to use the new facilities to bring education and business closer together to work collaboratively on cutting-edge renewable energy techniques'. This modern

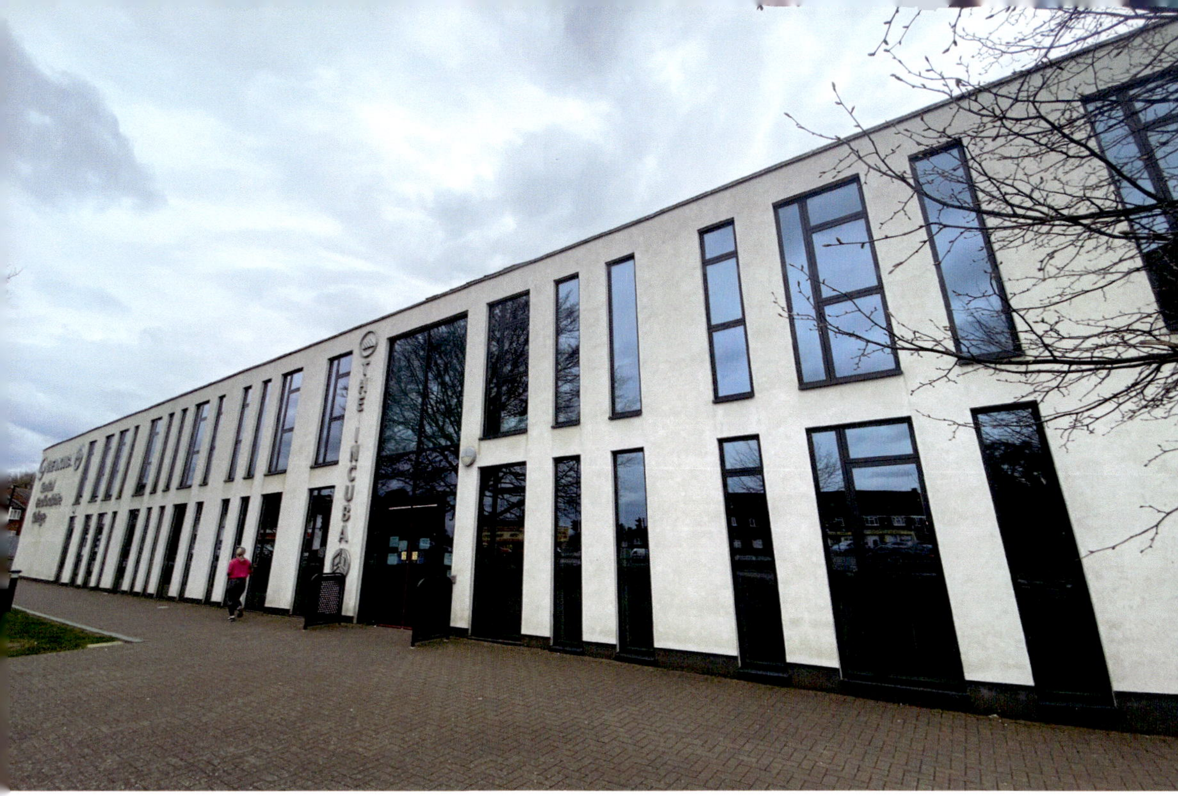

Above: The prominent Incuba building.

Right: Central Bedfordshire College's modern building, prominent as you come into Dunstable.

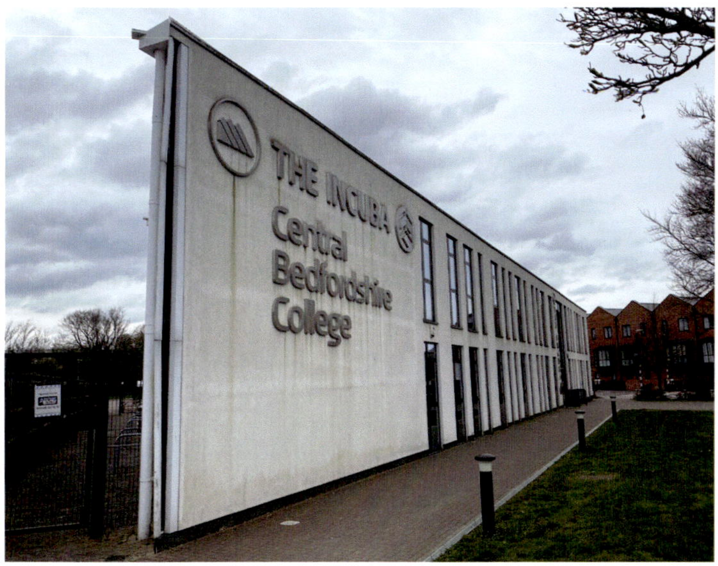

building is located on a former brownfield site at the corner of Brewers Hill on the busy A5 trunk road – you cannot miss it as you come into town.

The building itself was constructed using a highly insulated Metsec system, making the building very energy efficient. Photovoltaic panels and low-energy lighting were installed along with other environmentally friendly building systems, making the building sustainable in its use.

A Final Word from the Author

History surrounds us, from the landscapes we explore to the buildings we live, work or visit. Towns such as Dunstable are rich in history and many of these buildings are obvious to the eye, such as the priory and the many churches and civic buildings, but one of the most interesting aspects of searching out a building's history can start with a very small clue. For those interested in learning more about the places they live, I would urge you to look closer and start digging that bit deeper.

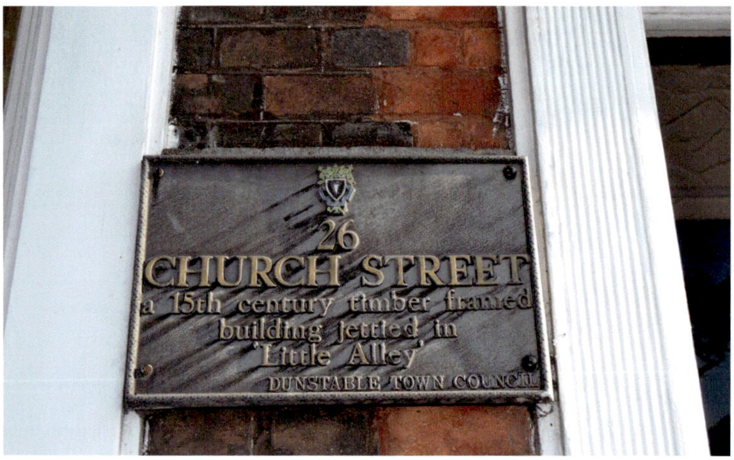

No. 26 Church Street, a little hint into its history.

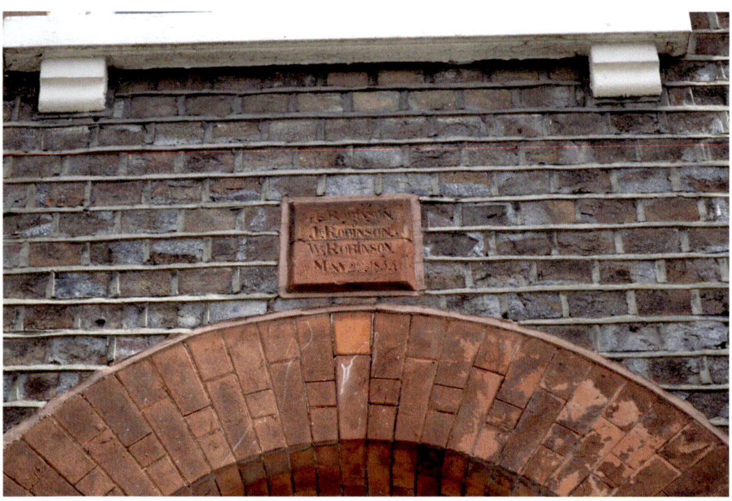

The tiniest clue can start an interesting journey into the history of a building.

Bibliography

Ancestry website for censuses
Various trade directories
Various websites for the many organisations cited within the book

Benson, Nigel C., *Dunstable in Detail* (The Book Castle: Dunstable, 1986)
Buckledee, John, *Dunstable Through Time* (Amberley Publishing: Stroud, 2014)
Dunstable Town Council – various Heritage Trail leaflets
Evans, Vivienne, *Dunstable with the Priory 1100–1550* (The Book Castle: Dunstable, 1994)
Evans, Vivienne, *Proud Heritage: A Brief History of Dunstable 1000–2000AD* (The Book Castle: Dunstable, 1999)
Old Dunstable: A Collection of Photographs (The Book Castle: Dunstable, 1975)
Smith, Worthington, G., *Dunstable: Its History & Surroundings* (The Homeland Association: London, 1904)
Walden, Richard *Streets Ahead: An Illustrated Guide to the Street Names of Dunstable* (The Book Castle: Dunstable, 1999)

Acknowledgements

As always, thanks to my ever-patient family for putting up with my frequent ramblings about all things historical and my sudden desire to head out with the camera because the sun was out and in the right location in the sky. I would also like to thank those who fed me information on the Historical Dunstable Facebook page, which was very useful – commiserations to those who suffered dental trauma at Chiltern House.

About the Author

Paul Rabbitts is a Fellow of the Royal Society of Arts, a Fellow of the Royal Historical Society, as well as a member of the Chartered Institute of Horticulture. He is a prolific author on local history, architecture, public parks and is an expert on the Victorian and Edwardian bandstand. He has written multiple books for the '50 Buildings' series including on Watford, Aylesbury, Leighton Buzzard, Luton, Hertford, Manchester, Salford, Welwyn and Welwyn Garden City, Carlisle, Bournemouth, Salisbury, Windsor and Tring. He is married and lives in Leighton Buzzard.